Collins

Bumblebee

A skill-based course on Environmental Studies

5

Dinu Raheja
Lipika Ghosh

Components of DigiSuite

Student + Teacher				Teacher-only	
a	animations	ia	activities	lp	lesson plans
ilt	instructor-led tutorials	w	worksheets	w	worksheets
g	games	v	videos	tn	teacher's notes
		audio	audio	ak	answer keys

Preface

Bumblebee is an innovative course on **Environmental Studies** for classes 1 to 5. It adopts a multidisciplinary approach to ensure holistic learning for young learners. An interactive and learner-centric course, ***Bumblebee*** has planned pedagogical elements as highlighted in the **National Education Policy, 2020** that imbue **21st Century Learning**, attitudes and values. These elements also help learners connect social, cultural and scientific concepts with real-life situations. Promoting experiential learning, learners are encouraged to explore their immediate world and foster environmental awareness.

The well-graded content has been created keeping in mind several goals—easy readability, accuracy and creativity. At the same time it empowers learners towards higher levels of academic scholarship.

Each chapter contains mindfully relevant questions and activities that hone **learning skills** such as creative thinking, critical thinking, problem-solving and communication; **literacy skills** and **life skills**. The content also provides opportunity to the students to enhance their **social-emotional learning**. Reflecting on their emotions or understanding the emotions of others will make the young learners feel confident from an early age to analyse and express their emotions.

Various relevant and critical issues related to the environment like pollution, plastic waste, recycling and climate change under the **United Nations Sustainable Development Goals (SDGs)** are addressed in the series. Activities based on these issues will extend learner's understanding and expression on these critical concerns.

The warm-ups and cross-curricular activities enrich learners with foundational literacy and numeracy to achieve competencies in reading, writing and numeracy as outlined in **NIPUN Bharat**.

The assessments track progress on core competencies under **Structured Assessment for Analyzing Learning Levels (SAFAL)** including the key stage assessment for Grade 5.

It is our endeavour to help the learners develop a responsible attitude towards the preservation of their environment.

- Authors

About the Authors

Dinu Raheja, an innovative educationist and administrator, recipient of the International Teacher's Award, has over 15 years of teaching experience in Indian and international schools. Formerly, Middle School Incharge, Sanskriti School, New Delhi, she is currently Director with The Global Education & Leadership Foundation (tGELF). Dinu also facilitates teacher and student leadership, entrepreneurship and 21st century skill development workshops.

Lipika Ghosh has over 25 years of teaching experience at St. Xavier's School Hazaribagh, Sardar Patel Vidyalaya, New Delhi and Sanskriti School, New Delhi. She has used innovative teaching methodology to make science a process of discovery interspersed with anecdotes for learners. Lipika has taught analytical skills and inculcated awareness of social issues amongst learners through science.

Key Features

Bumblebee is an innovative skill-based course on **Environmental Studies** for classes 1 to 5. The series focuses on **21st Century Learning** and inculcates in young learners the skills important to excel in the age of information.

- 21st century skills
- Experiential learning
- Social-emotional learning
- Happiness content
- Cross curricular
- Art integration
- United Nations Sustainable Development Goals
- Indian ethos

Bumblebee and NEP

Smart Skills — Life skills

Your parents are travelling, and you are excited as your grandparents are going to stay with you for a month. What are the things you will keep in mind to ensure that they feel comfortable and enjoy their stay?

Smart Skills
Helps students learn and demonstrate their ability for 21st century skills

Get Going

It was January 2020 when all of us and the entire world first heard of a new disease—the **coronavirus disease** or **COVID-19**. At that time no one imagined the extent of the crisis. The virus that causes this respiratory disease is called the coronavirus or SARS-CoV-2. It was first identified in December 2019 in Wuhan, China. A similar crisis called the Spanish Flu had occurred 100 years ago in the year 1919.

In March, the World Health Organization (WHO) declared a **Public Health Emergency**, and many countries along with India went into what none of us have experienced before—a lockdown. Everything closed for weeks all over India including trains, flights, restaurants, cinemas, even schools. People had to work from home. For students, their device became their school. Words like **masks, personal protective equipment (PPE), containment zones** and **social distancing** that were hardly used or heard of became commonplace.

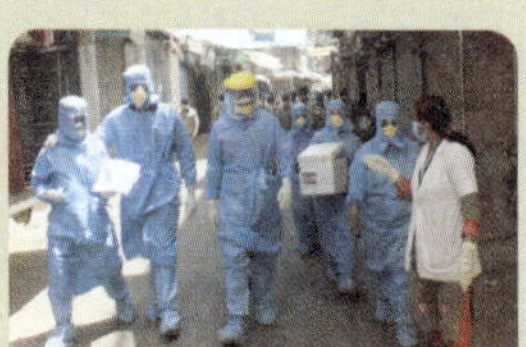

Covid-19 health team in Ahmedabad, India

Get Going
Stories, poems, interesting passages and quizzes promote reading and writing competencies as outlined in NIPUN Bharat

Skilling Up — Digital literacy

Shambu is an 8-year-old boy living in a village in Madhya Pradesh. His family has been displaced because of the dam construction on the river Narmada. His father has joined the Narmada Bachao Andolan. Research and find out about this movement. Make a PowerPoint presentation and share it in the class.

- What is the damage caused to the environment?
- How many people were displaced and in how many states by the dams constructed on the river?

What We Learnt

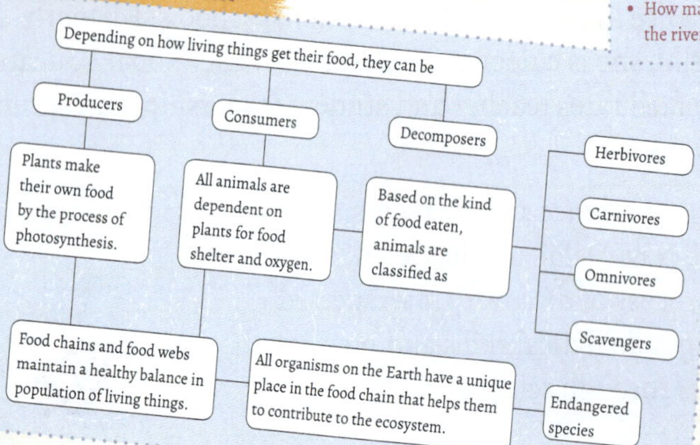

Skilling Up
Helps develop competencies for using the learnt skills

What We Learnt
Concept maps for comprehensive learning

Give It a Shot

12 RESPONSIBLE CONSUMPTION AND PRODUCTION

What do you do with your textbooks when you are promoted to the next class? Do you sell them to the *kabaadiwala*? As a class, donate your old textbooks to your juniors.

Instead of throwing your old notebooks, separate the unused pages from your notebooks and spiral bind them to use them for rough work in the new class. Sell the remaining copies to the *kabaadiwala* to recycle paper.

Picture Study

- What is the girl doing?
- How does it help us?

Give It a Shot
Activities for exploratory and experiential learning

Picture Study
Questions for inferential learning

Matter of Fact

Jatropha is a plant whose seeds are crushed, to produce jatropha oil which can be processed to produce a high- quality biodiesel. Biodiesel is used in a standard diesel car or further processed into jet fuel.

Matter of Fact
Interesting additional facts

Collins Bumblebee 5

Repurpose

Repurposing means using old things in different ways or modifying things to use them for something else.

Instead of throwing away clothes you outgrow, try to repurpose them.

Instead of throwing away greeting cards, calendars, posters, and cereal boxes, use them to make jigsaw puzzles.

Paper scraps or old paper can be pulped and used for making beautiful paper mache objects.

Before recycling try to repurpose!

Old yoga mats can be used as footpads and doormats.

Strips of old paper can be rolled, shaped and glued together to make jewellery or decorative items.

Old cardboard boxes can be decorated and used as storage boxes.

Make a Wall Garden

Step 1 Take some old bottles.

Step 2 Cut a bottle into half and punch small holes into it. Place a plant or a sapling in it.

Step 3 Hang the bottles in the garden or balcony, and your wall garden is ready.

Using the given materials design and draw your own balcony garden in the box. You can also paste a picture of your balcony.

Materials required: Empty plastic bottles of shampoo, oil containers or water bottles, empty coconut shell, old plastic bowls, wooden crates, old car tyres, soil, compost, seeds, plants and water.

Cross Connect

HC CC

- Hold a debate in class on the advantages and disadvantages of using alternative sources of energy.
- Draw, create and make an innovative vehicle of your imagination, which will work on alternative energy of your choice.

7 AFFORDABLE AND CLEAN ENERGY

Poster
Conservation of environment through application of the 5Rs

Cross Connect
Multidisciplinary activities to achieve various competencies as per NIPUN Bharat

Think and Answer
End-of-chapter exercises in multiple formats for inquiry and analysis-based learning

Suggested Assessments
Structured assessments designed as per SAFAL

Web link

For more information, log on to:

https://kids.nationalgeographic.com/pages/topic/ocean-portal

Last accessed 30 August 2021

Web links
Web links for extended learning

Table of Contents

1. My Family

Unit 1: My Family

Get Going

Inheritance of Traits

Gregor Mendel

Children often resemble one of their parents. A scientist named Gregor Mendel was the first person to study resemblances in family or **inherited** traits. While experimenting with pea plants in his garden, he found that the **inheritance** of certain traits in pea plants follows particular patterns. If the peas are yellow in colour, the baby plant would also have yellow peas. His experiments on more than 10,000 pea plants became the foundation of the study of heredity that showed we get some of our traits from our parents. It took him eight years to complete this study.

- You must have heard several times that you resemble one of your parents. Who do you resemble?
- What about you is similar to your parents?

Children often resemble their parents or family members. They may look like them or do something in exactly the same way as their mother or father. Although each one is unique, they share some **traits** with their family members which make them similar.

People, animals and plants pass certain **characteristics** to their young ones. This is why children often resemble their parents. These characteristics passed from one generation to another are called inherited or **hereditary** traits.

Children resemble their parents

traits: a particular quality in your personality; **characteristics:** features or qualities belonging typically to a person; **inherited:** to have qualities or physical features that are similar to those of your parents or grandparents

We get these characteristics or traits at birth. Traits are distinct qualities or characteristics that **distinguish** us from others. These can include hair colour, tooth shape, foot size, muscle structure and even likes and dislikes.

Traits are of two types—**acquired traits** and **hereditary** or **inherited traits**.

Matter of Fact

Twins are children born together to the same mother. They can be identical or fraternal. Identical twins inherit and share the same traits while fraternal twins inherit different traits from their parents.

Inherited traits

Inherited or hereditary traits are inherited from the parents and can be passed to the next generation. Eye colour, height, shape of the nose, dimples and even blood group are examples of inherited traits.

Give It a Shot

E

Did you inherit any traits from your grandparents, parents or other relatives? Make a family tree with as many of your relatives and generations as you can get information about. Try and paste pictures or draw them instead of just writing their names. Under each family member, mention their age and where they live. Also list the traits you have inherited against the relevant names.

Acquired traits

Acquired traits are **acquired** by people during their lifetime. These traits mainly refer to our behaviour, likes, dislikes and values. They cannot be passed down from one generation to another. For instance, we may not be able to inherit our parents' handwriting as it may have been acquired by them. Acquired traits also include lifestyle and food habits. Certain behaviours that help a person survive are also considered acquired.

We acquire many habits from our parents

distinguish: to notice a difference between people or things; **acquired:** learned or developed

Likes and Dislikes

Our likes and dislikes, for instance, the kind of clothes we like to wear, the movies we like to watch or even the sports we like to play, the food we eat, are **influenced** by our family, the people around us and the place where we grow up or live. We grow up following what we are taught and over time, these become our **habits**. Our family also helps shape our values, the way we behave, the way we speak and how we develop. Just think how your likes and dislikes have been influenced by your family. Is there anything you particularly like to do? Do you have a favourite colour that is also shared by someone in your family? Do you know your friends' likes and dislikes? Our food habits also get influenced by the place we are living in. We must respect the food habits of others. What is your favourite dish? What do you call it in your mother tongue? Can you tell the name of a dish being prepared just by its smell?

Smart Skills — Life skills (21ST CENTURY SKILLS)

Your parents are travelling, and you are excited as your grandparents are going to stay with you for a month. What are the things you will keep in mind to ensure that they feel comfortable and enjoy their stay?

Families help shape our values and habits

We are Unique

Each member of a family has several qualities that are unique to him or her. While we inherit and acquire some traits or qualities from our family, we also pick up many skills and habits from the environment in which we live. Several traits make us similar to our family, but there will be qualities that are unique to us. For instance, your favourite colour or your body is unique to you.

Smart Skills — Self-reflection (21ST CENTURY SKILLS)

Think about your qualities that you have inherited from your family or acquired from them or friends. Now, think about the qualities that are unique to you. Draw the given diagram in your notebook and complete it with your qualities, habits or traits.

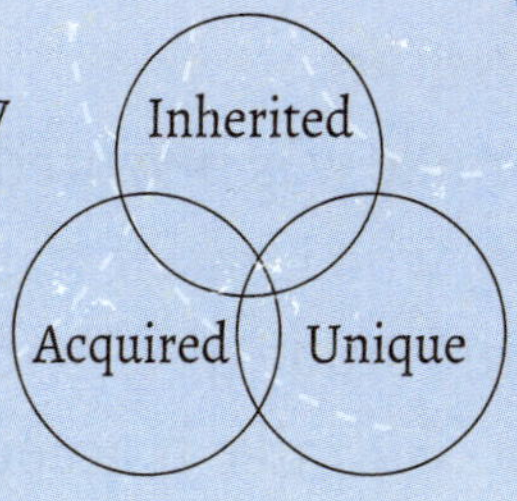

influenced: have an effect on

Relations

New relationships are formed once a child is born. People become mothers, fathers, grandmothers, grandfathers, brothers, sisters, aunts or uncles. Children grow well with the love and support of their family. The feeling of belonging and affection is important for the development of a child. Communicating well with each other in the family builds healthy relationships. In a happy family, each member contributes in making decisions, keeping in mind that every member's needs are met.

Feeling to Read

Every community is made up of people who have different needs. **Differently-abled people** are different from us. These are people who cannot see, speak or hear properly, and even those who cannot move freely on their own. Some others have difficulty in spelling words, reading or doing mathematical calculations.

Skilling Up

Critical thinking

21ST CENTURY SKILLS

- Older people who cannot hear very well, tend to speak loudly. Therefore, when we speak with them, we speak loudly too. Many of them wear a hearing-aid that helps them to hear better. How should we behave with these people?
- There are times and places when we are told not to speak loudly. Do you know when and where?

Sign language

There are some differently-abled who are unable to hear and speak. How do you think they communicate? They use sign language, communicating with the help of their fingers.

The Braille

The Braille was invented by the French educator, **Louis Braille**, who himself was blind. It helps the blind to read and study different subjects and achieve success in school. Braille is accepted as the only form of written communication for the blind all over the world.

Differently-abled people need care

Braille is a writing system that helps people **read by feeling** with their hands. It has six raised dots made in different combinations on paper that represent letters, punctuation marks and symbols. The hands recognise what the sequences of dots represent. By connecting the dots, words and sentences are formed. Braille is read by moving the hands from left to right along each line usually by using the first finger of both hands.

Smart Skills

Creative thinking and Collaboration

21ST CENTURY SKILLS

There are more than a hundred sign languages in the world. Many countries have their own sign language. Sometimes a specific sign language is used in schools which is known only to students of that school. In groups create your own sign language. Make a chart on this language. Remember to include facial expressions and body language. As a group enact the signs in class and let your classmates guess what you are trying to convey.

Did you know that many famous people in the world achieved success despite facing physical difficulties? **Ludwig van Beethoven**, the brilliant music composer could not hear. **Stephen Hawking**, a famous scientist, had many health issues yet he made some important discoveries in space research. **Helen Keller** was a famous author and teacher who could not see or hear.

Let us learn more about her.

The Story of Hellen Keller

Helen Keller could not hear, see or talk. She still studied and spent her life helping others. How do you think she could read? Helen Keller used Braille to read. In order to recognise the alphabet, she had to rely on her sense of touch.

Helen Keller's teacher, Anne Sullivan, taught Helen to read Braille. One day, she took Helen's hand and dipped it in water and spelt the word w-a-t-e-r on her palm. From then on, Helen learnt to read and write. Anne also taught her to speak. Helen had lost the ability to speak because she had not heard sounds for a long time. She touched her teacher's face and mouth when her teacher spoke and then she would touch her own face and mouth to say the same word. It was a slow and difficult process, but finally Helen began to speak.

Helen Keller

What We Learnt

Traits are distinct qualities or characteristics that distinguish us from others.

Traits are of two types—acquired traits and hereditary or inherited traits.

Acquired traits are learnt or acquired by us from the people around us or the place where we live.

Hereditary traits are inherited from both parents and can be passed down to the next generation.

All of us receive traits or characteristics from our parents.

While we inherit certain traits and characteristics from our family, we also have some qualities that make us unique.

Differently-abled people can do certain things which we cannot do.

Think and Answer

A. Fill in the blanks with the correct answers.

1. Characteristics passed from one generation to another are called ....
   a. acquired b. hereditary c. unique d. traits
2. My handwriting is a .... trait.
   a. inherited b. unique c. acquired d. none of these
3. People who cannot speak or hear communicate by using ....
   a. pen and paper b. Braille c. sign language d. facial expressions
4. Helen Keller was taught by her teacher ....
   a. Stephen Hawking b. Anne Sullivan c. Beethoven d. Albert Einstein
5. Disabled friendly buildings should have ....
   a. wide hallways b. ramps for wheelchairs
   c. lifts d. all of these

B. Fill in the blanks.

1. Distinct qualities and characteristics passed from one generation to another are called ....
2. Eating habits are greatly influenced by .... and ....
3. .... is a writing system that helps the blind to read by feeling with hands.

4. We .... some qualities from our parents and some from the place where we live.
5. Members of a family .... each other.

C. Match the following.

1.	Hair colour	a.	family traditions
2.	Born together	b.	acquired traits
3.	Likes and dislikes	c.	twins
4.	Eating habits	d.	inherited traits
5.	Skills	e.	make us unique

D. Answer these questions.

1. What is the difference between acquired and hereditary traits?
2. How do our family members influence our likes and dislikes?
3. Why do we resemble our parents?
4. How does braille help differently-abled people to read?
5. How did Ann Sullivan teach Helen Keller to speak?

Cross Connect

Work in two groups. A student from one group can volunteer to be blindfolded and another student can guide him or her. Make an obstacle path with a start and end point. Chairs, bags and bottles can be used as obstacles. Guide the blindfolded student through the path by giving directions to turn, stop or move. Observe how the student senses obstacles and makes his or her way without getting hurt.

Web link

For more information, log on to:
https://www.pbs.org/video/heredity-who-are-you-c7ngrj/

Last accessed on 30 August 2021

2. On the Move

Get Going

Migrant Workers

The COVID-19 pandemic brought the entire world to a lockdown. To stop the spread of the disease, India went into the largest lockdown, declared in March 2020, bringing life and everything else to a complete stop. Lakhs of workers and their families living and working in the cities started returning to their homes in the villages. For years migrant workers have been moving from their homes in the villages to the cities and urban areas to work as domestic help, at construction sites, in factories, as tailors, plumbers and day labourers in agriculture. They move in the hope of a better job, better salary and a better life. The lockdown did not just stop the trains, flights and buses, it also closed their places of work. With no money, unsure of when the lockdown will end or if they will still have a job, the migrant workers had no option but to return to their villages. This time the displacement was from the cities to the villages.

- What were some of the challenges faced by the workers on their journey home?
- Did their difficulties end when they reached their villages?

Thousands of people all over the world leave their homes for various reasons and settle in another city or country. This movement of people from one place to another is called **migration**.

Reasons for Migration

People migrate due to several reasons. Some people move to find better jobs and make a living in big cities. Poverty in the rural areas leads to migration from villages to nearby cities. Others move for better educational opportunities, for a better climate or for good healthcare. Sometimes, people also have to migrate because of natural calamities such as floods, drought, famine, war or outbreak of a disease. Forced migration is known as **displacement**.

displacement: removal of people to make place for something else

Rural poverty

Rural poverty is a major reason for migration. A large number of people in India live in villages and are farmers. However, not all of them own land. They are **landless farmers**. Such farmers work on other people's farms to earn a living. They do all the work on the fields like sowing the seeds, **harvesting** and **threshing**. They are **daily wage labourers** and get paid by the day. However, they do not earn enough money. When there is no work on the fields, these people travel far away from their fields, these people travel far away from their villages in search of work. They return to their villages only in time to sow or harvest the crops. Such migration is seasonal as it takes place only during certain seasons.

Picture Study

- When people move to cities in search of work where do you think they live?
- How is life in a village different from life in a city?

There are many **small farmers** who own small pieces of land which **yields** crops enough for their family. They usually have to borrow money from moneylenders at high **interest** rates to buy seeds, tools for agriculture, fertilisers and pesticides. In case the crop fails, either due to less or untimely rainfall or due to poor quality seeds, these farmers cannot repay their loans to the moneylenders. In fact, they borrow even more money for the next crop. As this cycle of borrowing money continues, the loan becomes so big that despite their earnings, they cannot fully repay the moneylender.

Smart Skills

Life skills

21ST CENTURY SKILLS

Imagine that your father is in a transferable job. The summer vacation has just ended and even as you are excited about meeting your school friends again, your mother informs you that you will be moving to another city and you would not be going back to school.

- How would you feel?
- How will you say bye to your friends?
- What are some of the difficulties you think you will face in a new city?

Most of these farmers are not aware of their rights and often get cheated by the moneylenders. In distress, many small farmers finally sell their land and migrate to cities in search of a better life.

harvesting: gathering agricultural crops; **threshing:** separating seeds from the plant; **yield:** produce; **interest:** the extra money that you pay back when you borrow money

Development Projects

Development projects like building of dams, highways, bridges or railway tracks also lead to displacement of people from their homes. Government officials **relocate** the villagers whose land and homes could be destroyed while constructing such structures. Although the villagers are relocated, often they cannot find jobs or cultivate crops on the new land, which may not be fertile. Faced with such situations, they migrate to nearby cities with their families in search of a better life. They feel that in the big cities their children will go to good schools and get a good education, they will get good jobs, freedom, safety and enough food to feed their families.

Skilling Up

Digital literacy — 21ST CENTURY SKILLS

1 NO POVERTY

Shambu is an 8-year-old boy living in a village in Madhya Pradesh. His family has been displaced because of the dam construction on the river Narmada. His father has joined the Narmada Bachao Andolan. Research and find out about this movement. Make a PowerPoint presentation and share it in the class.

- What is the damage caused to the environment?
- How many people were displaced and in how many states by the dams constructed on the river?

Way of Life

Some people have no permanent home. This is their way of life. **Gypsies** and **Banjaras** move from one place to another and are called **nomads**. They move for trade and new markets. They also move in search of fresh pastures for their cattle.

Banjara woman

Saperas and gujjars

Saperas or snake charmers are a semi-nomadic community. They are also snake catchers and are engaged to catch poisonous snakes. However, their means of livelihood has existed for many generations as snake charmers. They carry the snakes inside a round box made of cane and play a musical instrument called *been* or *pungi*. Its tune makes the snake move and sway as if it is dancing. However, snakes cannot hear sounds. For a snake, the person and the pungi are

Sapera

relocate: make a home in a new place; **nomads:** people who travel from place to place and do not have a permanent home

threats. Therefore, it responds to it as it would to a predator. Snake charmers sit outside the biting range. More drastic means of protection include removing the poisonous fangs or **plugging** them.

Gujjars

Gujjars are herders and cattle grazers who earn their livelihood by selling milk and butter. They depend on cows, buffaloes, sheep, camel and goats for these products. The women take care of the animals. They feed the cattle special kinds of leaves to get good quality milk. Found in Haryana, Rajasthan, Jammu and Kashmir and Himachal Pradesh, the Gujjars move with their cattle from mountains to the plains depending on the weather. Nowadays, because of deforestation and construction, pastures in villages have either shrunk or have disappeared completely.

Matter of Fact

There are about 500 nomadic groups in India totalling to about 80 million people. They can be broadly divided into three groups—hunter gatherers, cattle grazers and the craftsmen or trader groups. Of these the craftsmen-traders could be dancers, jugglers, snake charmers acrobats or fortune tellers.

Jobs on the move

How many of you know someone working in the defence forces? Those working in the defence forces like the army and air force also need to move to different cities or towns every two to three years. In such cases, the defence officers are posted in different cities and towns. While moving often might be routine for the officers, it can get very difficult for the family.

Give It a Shot

E

Making friends is not always easy. Adjusting to a new school and to a different city can be difficult. Work in groups and make a list of problems faced by children adjusting to a new school where they don't have any friends when their parents are transferred.

Conflict and Calamities

In 1947, India was divided into India and Pakistan. This partition was the biggest human movement in history. Millions of people in India and Pakistan were forced to leave their

plugging: blocking a snake's fangs with wax or any other material

homes, the people they knew, and at times even their families and belongings, to begin a new life on the other side of the border.

Refugee train during the partition of India

Effects of Displacement

Moving from one place to another can have both positive and negative effects. However, sometimes displacement can cause a lot of suffering to the people. Displaced people have to start their life all over again. Sometimes, they remain extremely poor and struggle to make ends meet. Migrant labourers are one such example. They mostly work at construction sites for a fixed period after which they migrate again. They do not have permanent homes and go through many difficulties. They should be given adequate support for their livelihood.

What We Learnt

People leave their homes and settle in another country or city for several reasons.

- Landless farmers do not have work throughout the year, they often migrate to cities in search of work.
- The farmers who own small pieces of land, often fall into debt and end up selling their land to move to other places.
- Construction of dams, bridges and railway tracks displaces many people.
- Gypsies and banjaras move from place to place for trade or new pastures for their cattle.
- Some people have to move due to transferable jobs like the defence forces.
- Natural calamities like earthquakes, cyclones, tsunamis and floods also causes people to leave their homes.

Think and Answer

A. Fill in the blanks with the correct answers.

1. People move from one place to another due to ....
   a. floods and famine b. better jobs c. education d. all of these
2. Landless farmers need to leave their villages in search of ....
   a. work b. homes c. education d. children
3. Villagers are relocated and their land is taken to build ....
   a. dams or bridges b. market place c. multi-storey d. farm buildings

4. .... have no permanent homes.
   a. Businessmen b. Pilots c. Banjaras d. Doctors
5. .... have transferable jobs.
   a. Farmers b. Defence forces c. Gypsies d. Moneylenders

B. Fill in the blanks.

1. Gypsies are also called .... and ....
2. People move from one place to another for ....
3. Farmers who do not have their own fields are called ....
4. Government officials .... people whose homes are destroyed while laying railway tracks.
5. Movement of people from one place to another is known as ....

C. Write *T* for true or *F* for false.

1. People who move from one country to another to settle down are known as labourers. ☐
2. Many people become homeless during a natural disaster. ☐
3. Projects like the building of dams or bridges lead to displacement of people. ☐
4. The partition of India was the biggest human movement in history. ☐
5. Daily wage workers get paid once in a month. ☐

D. Answer these questions.

1. How does the building of a dam or bridge affect the people living in the area?
2. Why do small farmers who own land need to migrate?
3. What kind of migration do landless farmers undertake? Why do they need to migrate?
4. Who are the gypsies? Why are they called nomads?
5. List some of the reasons why people move.

Cross Connect

Interview your grandparents. Find out where their ancestors came from. Did they witness the Partition of India? How did they choose whether to live in Pakistan or Bangladesh or move to India? Were they able to carry everything they had in their homes with them? What about their friends? What was it like for them to leave their homes and friends and move to a strange and new city? Create a photo gallery of old photos and bring to class for a Show and Tell.

Web link

For more information, log on to:
https://www.bbc.co.uk/newsround/46428985

Last accessed on 30 August 2021

3. A Natural Balance

Get Going

What do we get from plants and animals? Name and draw their pictures in the box.

Plants	Animals

Imagine a world either without plants or without animals. What is more important?

All living things need food to survive. Animals are dependent on plants for food, shelter and oxygen while green plants make their own food. Both plants and animals eat different types of food and acquire it in different ways. Plants respire just like us. They breathe in oxygen and breathe out carbon dioxide throughout the day and at night. At night, plants stop making food and release only carbon dioxide. As the Sun appears, the plants start making their food and releasing oxygen. Thus, the amount of oxygen released is more in the daytime, which is beneficial for all living beings.

Food for Plants

Plants need sunlight, carbon dioxide and water to live.

Green plants

Green plants are called **producers** because they make their own food. The process by which green plants make their food in the presence of chlorophyll, sunlight, carbon dioxide and water is known as **photosynthesis**. It takes place in the leaves.

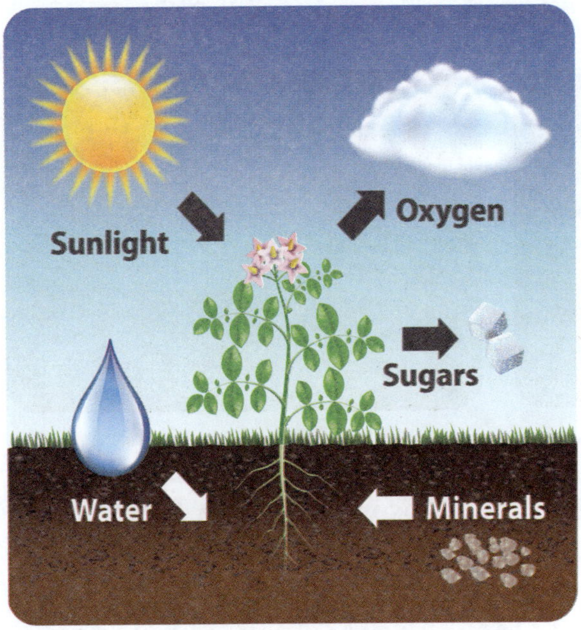

Photosynthesis

Picture Study

Do you know how and where do the plants make their food?

During photosynthesis, green plants absorb energy from the Sun. This energy is absorbed with the help of a **pigment** called **chlorophyll**, which is present in all green leaves. Water and minerals are absorbed by the roots and are carried to other parts of the plant. Carbon dioxide is absorbed through tiny **pores** in the leaves called stomata. Sunlight, water and carbon dioxide are used to make food in the form of **glucose** or sugar and oxygen is released into the air.

Smart Skills

Life skills

21ST CENTURY SKILLS

Gift potted plants or saplings to your friends or relatives on birthdays or other occasions and encourage them to do the same. Write a message on a card and give it along with the potted plant.

The following reaction explains the process of photosynthesis.

$$\text{Carbon dioxide + Water} \xrightarrow[\text{Chlorophyll}]{\text{Sunlight}} \text{Sugar + Oxygen}$$

A portion of the glucose is used by plants for their growth. The remaining glucose is stored as **starch** in different parts of the plant such as roots, stems, leaves, seeds and fruits. Some vegetables like potato and tapioca are rich in starch. Plants obtain nutrients from the soil. Over time, these nutrients run out and need to be replaced. Therefore, gardeners add manure and fertilisers to the soil.

pigment: a natural substance that gives a plant or an animal its colour; **pores:** small holes on the surface of a plant or a rock; **glucose:** a substance which is an important source of energy

Parasitic plants

Plants that obtain nutrition by growing on other plants are called **parasitic plants**. The plants on which the parasitic plants feed are called **host plants**. Parasitic plants attach themselves firmly to the stems or roots of the host plant to absorb nutrients. Mistletoe, *Rafflesia*, dodder (Amarbel) or *Cuscuta* are some parasitic plants. Non-green plants like mushrooms, mosses and some fungi depend on other plants for food.

Rafflesia

Cuscuta

Smart Skills — Digital literacy — 21st Century Skills

Name two parasitic plants other than those in the chapter. Where are they found? How do parasitic plants harm the host plants? Discuss in class.

Carnivorous or insectivorous plants

Plants that obtain nutrition by eating small animals such as insects, flies and bugs are called **carnivorous** or **insectivorous plants**. They grow in soil that lacks certain nutrients like nitrogen. They trap insects to get nitrogen. Carnivorous plants digest their prey using **enzymes**. The pitcher plant, sundew plant and Venus flytrap are some carnivorous plants.

The pitcher plant looks like a pitcher with a lid. It has hair and nectar inside that attracts insects. As soon as an insect sits on it, the lid closes, thus trapping the insect. The Venus flytrap has jaw-like leaves with spiky teeth along the edges. Sundew plants have a gel-like sticky substance that covers the leaf. Insects easily get stuck to the plant and become prey.

Venus flytrap

starch: a substance found in many plants which acts as a store of energy; **derive:** obtain something from; **enzyme:** a substance produced by a living thing that aids in digestion of food

Smart Skills

Information literacy

21ST CENTURY SKILLS

Epiphytes are plants that grow on another plant or an object for physical support. Orchids, mosses, and ferns are epiphytes. They derive moisture and nutrients from the air, rain, water—in marine environments—or from the waste accumulating around it. Epiphytes are not parasitic on the supporting plants. Find out if epiphytes harmful to the plants. Give reasons.

Food for Animals

All animals are consumers as they depend on plants as well as on other animals for food. Based on the kind of food they eat, animals can be classified as **herbivores**, **carnivores**, **omnivores**, **scavengers** and **decomposers**. Animals who feed only on plants are known as herbivores. Cows, deer, elephants and goats are herbivores. Animals who feed on other animals are called carnivores. They depend indirectly on plants for their food. Lions, tigers, leopards and wolves are carnivores. Animals who feed on both plants and animals are called omnivores. Crows, cockroaches and bears are omnivores.

Some animals help to keep the environment clean by eating dead animals. They are called scavengers. Hyenas, vultures and crows are examples of scavengers.

Some organisms obtain their food by consuming dead and decaying plants and animals. They are called decomposers. Bacteria, **fungi** and earthworms are examples of decomposers. All dead plants and animals are recycled in nature by the decomposers that help release nutrients from them into the soil, which are then used by plants for nutrition.

Fungi

Interdependence

Interdependence is when two or more living organisms depend on each other. Plants and animals depend on each other for various needs. Plants depend on animals for carbon dioxide, insects such as bees and birds help in seed dispersal and earthworms help to make the soil fertile for plant growth. Animals and human beings depend on plants for food and oxygen. Some animals depend on plants for shelter. Human beings also depend on plants for other needs such as clothes, medicines, petroleum and wood.

organism: an individual animal or a plant; **fungi:** a living thing that is similar to a plant without leaves, flowers or green colouring, and that usually grows on plants or on decaying matter

Skilling Up

Critical thinking

21ST CENTURY SKILLS

- Why should we not sleep under a tree at night?
- What will happen if the number of carnivores is more than that of herbivores?

Food Chain

A **food chain** is the chain formed when plants are eaten by animals and then these animals are eaten by other animals. It shows how energy is passed from the Sun to producers, from producers to consumers, and from consumers to decomposers. Plants are eaten by herbivores, which in turn, are eaten by carnivores. When carnivores die, they are consumed by decomposers. The concept of food chain was coined by an English scientist, **Charles Elton** in 1927. Let us study the following food chains to understand this better.

Food chain on land

A rabbit eating grass is an example of a simple food chain.

Grass ⟶ Rabbit

In the following food chain, grass is eaten by a deer, which in turn is eaten by a lion.

Grass ⟶ Deer ⟶ Lion

In a longer food chain, a grasshopper who eats grass, is eaten by a frog, which is then eaten by a snake. Finally, the snake is eaten by an eagle.

Grass ⟶ Grasshopper ⟶ Frog ⟶ Snake ⟶ Eagle

Aquatic food chain

In a pond or a river, the food chain starts with aquatic plants such as **algae** because they are producers. Snails feed on algae and are then eaten by fish. Fish are eaten by cranes.

Food Web

A food chain does not exist independently in nature. Different **interconnected** food chains form a **food web**.

Organisms of one food chain can be eaten by different organisms of another food chain. Let us understand this with the help of an example. Plants are eaten by herbivores such as grasshoppers, rabbits and deer. Herbivores are eaten by many carnivores such as tigers, lions and wolves. In the same way, lions can eat deer, rabbits, zebras and cows.

algae: very small living organisms that exist in groups mostly in water or moist areas; **interconnected:** having linked parts

Food chains and food webs maintain a **natural balance** in the population of living things on the Earth. Animals, plants, birds and marine **species** are as important as human beings. If the population of one organism increases or decreases, the entire food chain gets disturbed.

Food web

Give It a Shot

E

In groups of four, observe the animals, birds and insects that live in your neighbourhood and write down their names. Draw one food chain and a food web to explain their interdependence.

Extinction of Living Organisms

All organisms on the Earth have a unique place in the food chain that helps them contribute to the ecosystem. An **ecosystem** is a community of interacting organisms and their physical environment. However, many animals, plants and birds are endangered. An **endangered species** is an animal or plant species that is in danger of becoming **extinct**, that is, its number is decreasing rapidly. This happens because of an increase in the number of **predators**, climate change or loss of natural habitat.

Matter of Fact

The golden toad was the first species to become extinct as a direct result of climate change. Also called the orange toad, it was discovered about 56 years ago by a **zoologist** Jay Savage in 1964. Male golden toads are orange while females show a greater variety of colour, including black, yellow, red, green and white.

species: a group of closely related organisms that are like each other; **zoologist:** a scientist who studies animals; **extinct:** no longer alive; **predator:** an animal that naturally preys on others

What We Learnt

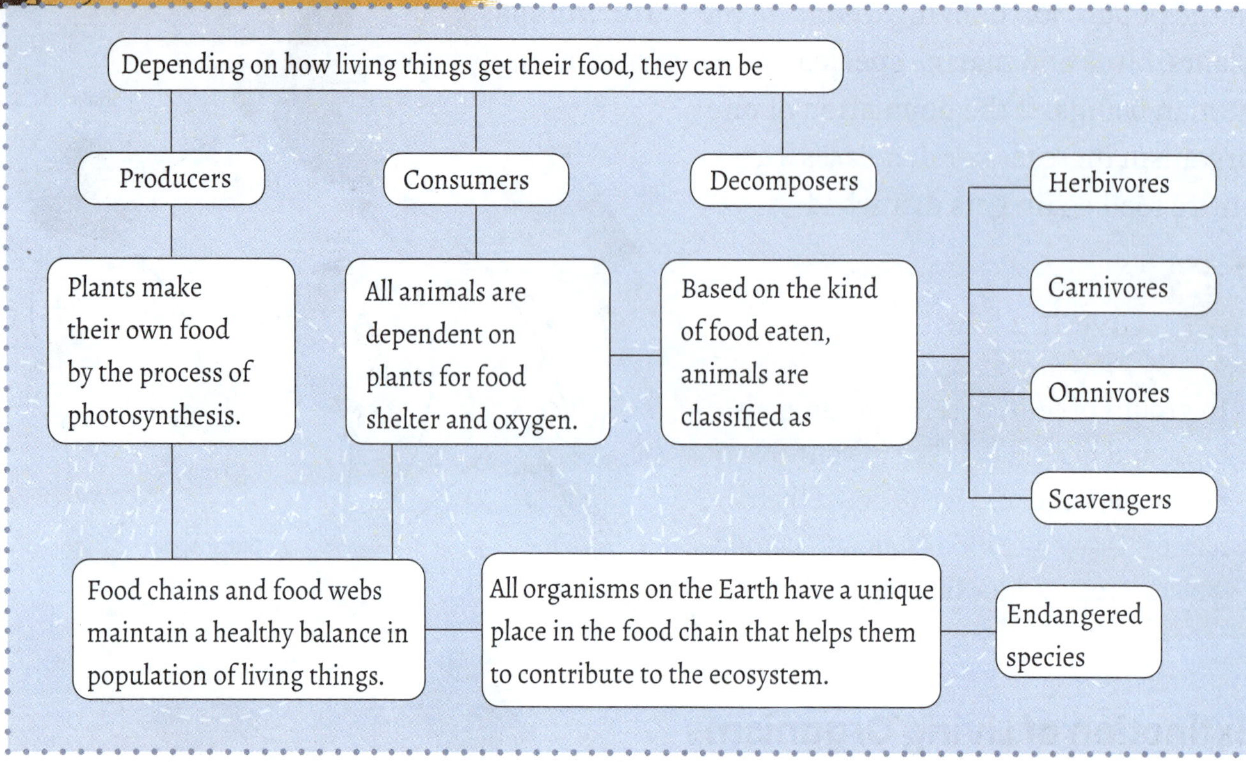

Think and Answer

A. Fill in the blanks with the correct answers.

1. .... are called producers.
   a. Herbivores b. Bacteria c. Omnivores d Green plants
2. Plants absorb energy from sunlight with the help of ....
   a. stomata b. oxygen c. chlorophyll d. water
3. A .... is an omnivore.
   a. tiger b. snake c. bear d. sheep
4. .... help to recycle nutrients into the nature.
   a. Producers b. Decomposers c. Carnivores d. Scavengers
5. Animals that eat dead animals are called ....
   a. decomposers b. producers c. consumers d. scavengers

B. Name the following.

1. Two herbivores ...., ...
2. Two parasitic plants .... , ...
3. Two carnivorous plants .... , ...
4. Two decomposers .... , ...
5. Two scavengers .... , ...

C. Write *T* for true and *F* for false.

1. Crows and vultures are scavengers.
2. In a food chain, the energy comes from plants.
3. Producers are at the end of the food chain.
4. Plants do not make their own food.
5. Carnivorous plants digest their prey using enzymes.

D. Answer these questions.

1. What is photosynthesis?
2. What are parasitic plants?
3. What is a food chain and a food web? Explain with the help of an example.
4. What do you understand by balance in nature?
5. What are the causes of extinction of plants and animals?

Cross Connect

HC CC

Form two groups. Hold each other's hands and form two circles. The objective of this game is to untangle yourself without letting go of any hands. Start by standing in a small circle without holding hands.

How to play:

- Hold the hand of the player standing next to you.
- With your other hand hold the hand of another player in the circle who is not standing next to you.
- At the end of the game, all players should be standing once again in a circle, without any players left in the centre.

Getting untangled requires clear communication and cooperation. Players may readjust their grip to be more comfortable while playing.

Make it interesting

- Add restrictions to communication methods.
- Make it a 10-minute activity.

Web link

For more information, log on to:
https://kids.nationalgeographic.com/awesome-8/article/carnivorous-plants

Last accessed on 30 August 2021

4. Plant Story

Unit 2: Plants and Animals

Get Going

Who brought coffee to India?

Coffee originated in Ethiopia, a country in Africa. The plant was exported to other parts of the world. Coffee grows on large areas called **plantations**. Ripe coffee berries are picked and then dried. The seeds, also called beans, are taken out and roasted in varying temperatures. The darker the colour of the coffee beans, the stronger is the coffee. It is believed that a Sufi saint, Baba Budan, introduced the coffee plant to India. He brought the seeds from a country called Yemen and grew them near his home in Mysore. The coffee-producing regions of India are Karnataka, Kerala, Tamil Nadu and some parts of Andhra Pradesh.

- Name two states where coffee is produced?
- Which kind of coffee do your parents drink? Name them.

Plants, like all living things, grow. Small baby plants grow to become tall plants and trees. Let us find out how plants grow and the things they need to grow. Growing plants is important, as our life largely depends on them. Most plants are grown from seeds. Flowers change into fruits and fruits have seeds inside them. Seeds grow into new plants. Before we learn about the growth of a seed, let us learn about the structure of a seed.

Structure of a Seed

The structure of the bean seed can be observed by soaking it overnight. A seed has an outer covering called the **seed coat** or **testa**. Its function is to protect the baby plant inside.

There is a tiny hole in the seed called **micropyle** through which the seed absorbs water. Each half of a seed is called a **seed leaf** or a **cotyledon**. It stores food for the developing baby plant.

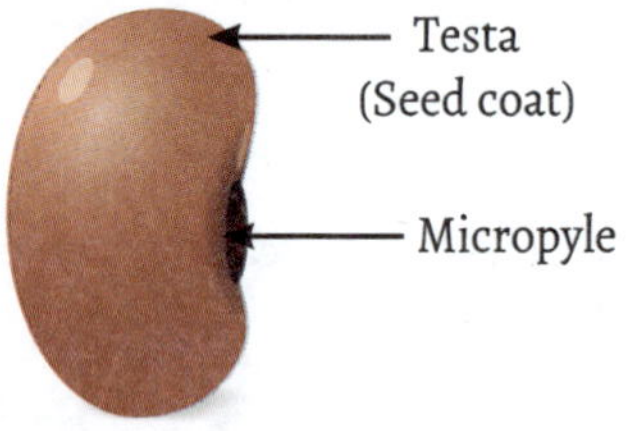

Bean seed

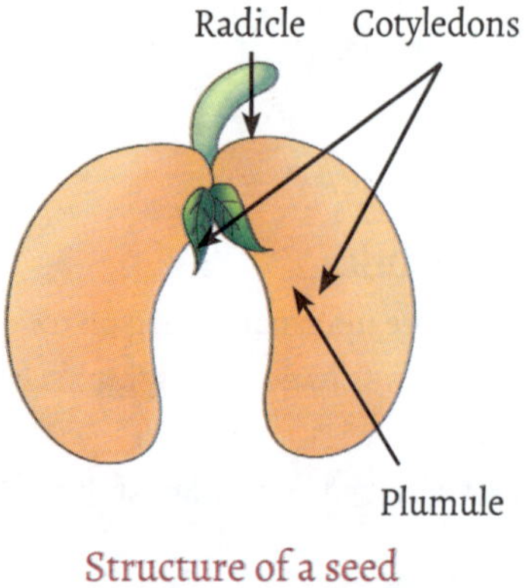

Structure of a seed

The baby root is called the **radicle** and baby shoot is called **plumule**. When a seed sprouts, the cotyledons are the first leaves that the plant has. Some plants have one cotyledon while others have two. An **embryo** is a baby plant inside the seed. It grows into a new plant.

Skilling Up Communication 21ST CENTURY SKILLS

Discuss in the class about edible seeds, nutritious seeds and oil-producing seeds with examples.

Seed Germination

If seeds get the right amount of water, air, sunlight and warmth, they produce a baby plant called **seedling**. The process by which a seed grows into a baby plant or a seedling is called **germination**.

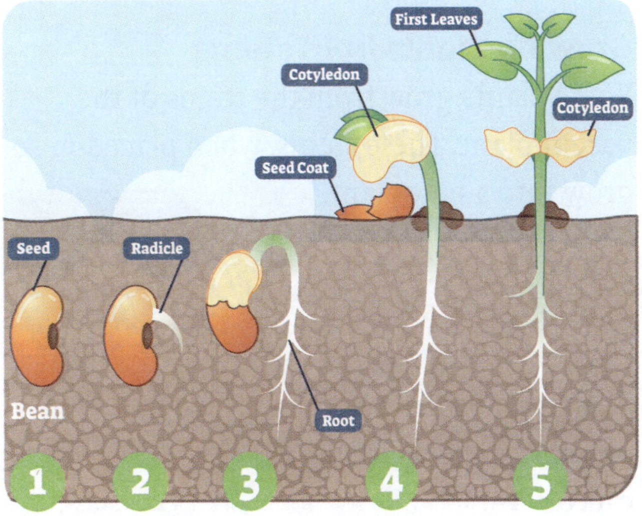

Seed germination

Water helps to soften the seed coat and changes the food stored in the cotyledons into a soluble substance. Baby plant uses this soluble food to grow. Warmth from sunlight speeds up the growth of the baby plant and air provides it energy to sprout. Some seeds remain **dormant**, that is, they do not germinate until the growing conditions are suitable. When a seed sown in soil gets enough warmth, air, sunlight and water, the seed coat breaks.

The **radicle** is the first part of the embryo which comes out through the micropyle of the seed. It grows further and forms the **root system** of the plant. As the seed germinates the plumule grows above the ground and forms the **shoot system**. As the roots and the shoot grow, leaves grow bigger and the cotyledons shrink and eventually, fall off.

Give It a Shot

E

Soak chickpeas overnight. Take three containers and mark them as A, B and C. Place a moist cotton cloth in container A and place a few soaked seeds on it. In container B, place a few dry seeds and fill it with water. Put some dry seeds in container C. Place all the three containers in a place where they get sunlight and air. Cotton in container A should always be kept moist. Observe the seeds for four days and note down your observations for each day in a tabular form in your notebook. What do you think happened to the seeds in the three containers? In which container, did the seeds sprout and why?

dormant: alive but not actively growing

How Plants Grow

Many plants reproduce through seeds. However, some plants reproduce from their **vegetative parts**. Stems, roots and leaves are the vegetative parts of a plant. Let us find out how plants grow from these parts.

Picture Study

- Do all plants grow from seeds?
- Do you know of plants growing into a new plant other than seed? Name them.

Growing plants from stems

Some plants grow from the stems of the parent plant. These stems, when placed in soil, grow into a new plant.

Potato and ginger are **underground stems**. They grow into new plants from small buds present on their surface called **eyes**.

Potato buds

Some plants grow from **stem cuttings**. A piece of the stem of the parent plant is cut and planted in the soil. The stem cutting produces new roots and grows into a new plant. Rose, money plant and hibiscus are grown using stem cuttings.

Stem cuttings

Growing plants from roots

Sweet potato, carrot, radish and turnip are roots of plants that store food. The top portion of the carrot and the roots of turnip when planted in soil, grow into new plants from their roots.

Root cutting

Growing plants from leaves

In plants such as *Begonia* and *Bryophyllum*, young plants can grow from well-developed leaves, while these leaves are still attached to the branch. **Young plants** are found on the edges of the leaf. Once these young plants develop, they drop-off or detach themselves from the parent plant. They grow into new plants in moist soil.

Bryophyllum

Growing plants from spores

In some plants, such as ferns, mushrooms and mosses, new plants grow from **spores**. Spores are very light and tiny powdery structures. In ferns, spores are present on the back of the leaves as brown rings.

Fern spores

Smart Skills — Life skills

21ST CENTURY SKILLS

Make your own kitchen garden

Plant tomato, green chilli, coriander, fenugreek seeds in small pots, water them and keep them in sunlight. What happens? Bring the pots or click pictures and share it in the class. Write the names of green chilli, fenugreek, cumin, cloves, cardamom, coriander, cinnamon in Hindi and two more Indian languages.

Dispersal of Seeds

Smart Skills — Information literacy

21ST CENTURY SKILLS

Find out which is the largest seed in the world. What is its length? Where is it found?

If seeds are sown very close to each other, they struggle for space, light, air, water and nutrients. Therefore, it is necessary that seeds are **scattered** far away from each other. The process by which seeds travel or are scattered far away from the parent plant is called **dispersal of seeds**. Seed dispersal is carried out by wind, water, animals and explosion.

Dispersal by wind

Some plants have light and hairy or wing-shaped seeds that get easily blown away to far-off places. Dandelion and cotton seeds are dispersed by wind.

Dandelion

Dispersal by water

The seeds of some plants have a waterproof covering. They can float on water and are carried to far-off places. For example, coconut has a fibrous covering that helps it float on water. When it washes up ashore, new plants grow out of it. Seeds of the lotus plants are spongy and float on water. Water lily seeds are also designed to float.

Water lily seeds

Matter of Fact

The Clark's nut cracker's staple diet is pine seeds. It uses its sharp, long and sturdy beak to crack open pinecones and carries the seeds to a distance. It often buries these seeds at the perfect depth for germination, and in due time seeds sprout and grow into new trees.

scattered: thrown in various directions

Dispersal by animals

Sheep with cocklebur

Some seeds have hook-like structures that help them cling on to animals' fur. Similarly, some seeds have sticky substances that help them stick to animals' skin. This way, the seeds are carried away from the parent plant. Fruits like mangoes, oranges, lychees and apples are eaten by animals, birds and humans. Their seeds are thrown away, which grows into a new plant.

Many birds and animals eat fruits along with their seeds. The seeds come out of their bodies in their droppings and are scattered in different places where they grow into new plants. Seeds of cocklebur, guava and berries are dispersed by animals.

Pea

Dispersal by explosion

Many fruits burst with a sudden jerk as a result the seeds are scattered on all sides, far away from the parent plant. This mechanism of seed dispersal is called explosion. Examples of plants whose seeds are dispersed by **explosion** are pea, poppy, balsam and castor.

Smart Skills — Critical thinking (21st Century Skills)

What would the world look like if there were no seeds? What would the birds eat? Discuss.

Some Plants and their Places of Origin

The story of tea

Tea was first discovered in China. Shennong, a healer and ruler of ancient China, one day tasted a mixture of dried leaf and boiling water and liked it. Thus, he discovered tea, and that it can be used as medicine. Tea was brought to India by the British. Today, India is one of the largest tea producers in the world.

Tea plantation

Tea shrubs require mountain soil rich in humus and needs well-drained land and heavy rainfall. Mountain slopes are good for growing tea as water does not flood the soil. Only the top layers of the mature plant are picked. These buds and leaves are called flushes. A plant grows a new flush every seven to fifteen days during the growing season. These are dried and processed into tea.

The story of fiery Chinar

Chinars

The Chinar is a huge tree **native** to Greece. In India, the tree grows in the Himalayan region. However, most of them are found in Kashmir. It is believed that the Mughals planted these beautiful trees in Kashmir.

The Chinar is called *buen* in the Kashmiri language. The leaves are green in summer and change their colour to a blazing yellowish-brown in autumn. The emperor Jahangir planted chinar in Shalimar Garden which trees still exist as chinars can live for more than 300 years. They have distinct leaves that look much like the leaves of a maple tree. Four Chinar trees called 'Char Chinar' grow in the middle of the Dal Lake.

Some Plants and their Places of Origin			
Plant	**Origin**	**Plant**	**Origin**
Corn	Mexico	Potato	South America
Chillies	Mexico	Watermelon	South Africa
Onion	Egypt	Lemon	Europe
Cucumber	China	Mango	India

What We Learnt

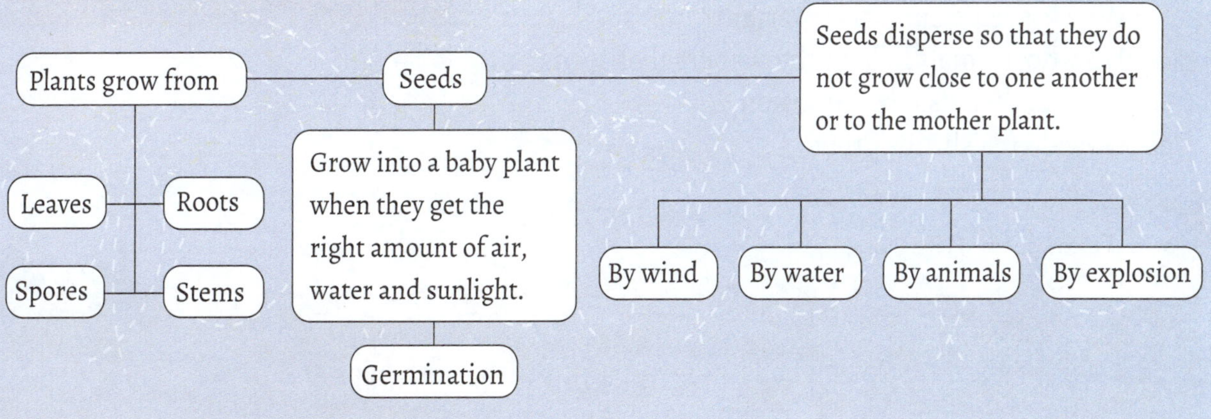

Think and Answer

A. Fill in the blanks with the correct answers.

1. The .... (seed coat/cotyledons/micropyle) stores food for the baby plant.
2. The seeds of .... (poppy/dandelion/water lily) disperse through wind.

native: connected with the place where you were born

3. The .... (stem/roots/leaves) of Bryophyllum grow new plants.
4. Potato is a .... (root/stem/leaf).
5. .... (Haryana/Punjab/Kerala) is coffee producing region of India.

B. Name the following.

1. A seed that is dispersed by water ....
2. A tiny hole through which a seed absorbs water ....
3. The process of seed dispersal in which fruits burst open ....
4. A baby plant inside the seed ....
5. Seed leaves are known as ....
6. Chinar in Kashmiri language is ....

C. Write *T* for true and *F* for false.

1. Seeds germinate in the presence of water, air, sunlight and warmth. ☐
2. Seeds of some plants have a waterproof coating and can float. ☐
3. Plants can grow only from stem cuttings. ☐
4. Potato and ginger are roots. ☐
5. The part of the plant that grows above the ground is called the shoot system. ☐
6. Chillies or chilli peppers originally grew in Portugal. ☐

D. Answer these questions.

1. What does a seed need to germinate?
2. Explain the process of germination of a seed.
3. Why is seed dispersal important?
4. How do animals help in the dispersal of seeds?
5. Explain dispersal by explosion.
6. How do tea shrubs grow?

Cross Connect

Paint a Chinar or Maple tree!

Materials required: Cotton balls, paints, paint brush, cloth pegs and paper

- Paint the sky blue on the drawing paper and let it dry.
- Draw out their branches and paint them.
- Use red, orange, yellow colour to paint the leaves, use cotton balls.
- Make a Chinar tree or Maple tree on the paper with paints.

Web link

For more information, log on to:
https://www.natgeokids.com/uk/discover/science/nature/the-life-cycle-of-flowering-plants/

Last accessed on 30 August 2021

5. The Awesome Five

Get Going

Sniffer Dogs

We all know about our five main senses: sight, hearing, smell, taste and touch. Animals also have senses, to detect what is happening around. When compared to many animals, human eyes see in detail a wide range of colours. However, some animals have more highly developed senses than us, such as hearing and smell. Police forces have found that dogs have a highly developed sense of smell. The dogs are trained to detect specific scents from human body, or odour from drugs. Dog breeds with best sense of smell are trained. Sniffer dogs are used to detect different crimes.

- Have you seen sniffer dogs? Where? Which breed?
- Do you know where else they are used?

We know the world through our senses of sight, smell, taste, hearing and touch. These help us to enjoy our food, listen to music, see and feel things and recognise different types of smells. In other words, our senses help us understand the world around us.

Animal Senses

Like humans, animals too have sense organs. Sense organs help animals find food, escape from their enemies or **predators**, communicate with each other and find others of their kind. In animals, one particular sense is more developed than the others. Animals rely on the most developed sense to get food and escape from danger.

Skilling Up

Knowledge-based

21ST CENTURY SKILLS

- Why do you think snakes sway to the tune played by snake charmers?
- Do you know of an instance where an animal has helped a human? How?

predator: an animal that kills and eats other animals

Sense of smell

Many animals have a keen sense of smell. Dogs have an excellent sense of smell. They can find hidden things by their sense of smell. They are trained by the police to find criminals, crime scene evidence, missing people, **illegal** substances, and dangerous bombs and attacking people targeted by police. Ants too have an excellent sense of smell. Ants have special sense organs called **antennae** on their heads that they use to smell, to find their way and to follow each other. Hence, we see them gathered around sweet food items such as jam, sugar and doughnuts. Bees, butterflies and flies also have these special organs. The forked tongue of a snake can collect smells from two different places at the same time. A stronger smell also helps the snake with a sense of direction.

Picture Study

- Do you have pet dogs?
- Have you noticed how they sit by the table when you are eating your food?
- How do they know it is meal time?

Smart Skills

Information literacy

21st CENTURY SKILLS

Talk to children who have pets. Find out how do they understand the actions of their pets. Make a list of all answers in a tabular form and see the similarity between the actions of the animals.

Sense of taste

The tongue is vital for tasting food and for talking. Humans taste with their tongue; however, butterflies, bees and houseflies taste with their feet. A butterfly walks on the leaves of the plant before laying eggs on it. This is done to make sure that it is edible for the caterpillar when it hatches. Snakes, some lizards and cats also smell with their tongues.

There are no taste buds on the tongue of a snake. They have what is called a **Jacobson's Organ** on the roof of their mouths. They **flick** their tongues in the air to smell and taste

illegal: not permitted by law; **antennae:** a pair of long, thin feelers on the heads of insects

and when the tongue is brought back into the mouth, it is placed on the Jacobson's Organ and interpreted by the brain as a taste or a smell. Ants also have a sharp sense of taste and can tell sour, sweet, bitter and salty tastes. Whenever ants find food, they leave a **trail** of chemicals on the ground, which other ants follow to reach the food.

Snake

Sense of sight

Eyes have lens that help us to see. When we see something, the lens in each eye forms an image on the back of the eye. This sends a message to the brain. The brain reads the message and tells us what we are seeing.

Birds have powerful eyesight because their eyes are bigger as compared to the size of their heads. Their large eyes produce a large image that helps them see even while they are flying. A bald eagle can spot a mouse in a field while flying high. Cheetahs and tigers have sharp eyesight. They can spot their prey from afar and see at night.

Eagles have sharp eyesight

All **nocturnal animals** have large eyes that gives them good night vision. They depend on their sense of hearing as well. Owls have large eyes that help them hunt at night. Although their eyes are fixed in their sockets, their necks are flexible and can turn all the way around.

Ants, flies and mosquitoes have **compound eyes**. This means that they have many tiny lenses attached together. This helps them see in many directions at the same time. It is thus difficult to catch a fly or a mosquito.

Compound eyes

Ducks have a transparent **membrane** that covers their eyes when they dive into water. This prevents their eyes from getting wet and helps them see under water. Some birds and bees can see colours that human beings cannot see. Dogs and cats have very poor colour vision. They can usually see objects in shades of grey, blue or yellow.

flick: to make sudden, quick movements; **trail:** a long line of marks left behind; **nocturnal animals:** animals that are active at night; **membrane:** a thin layer of skin that covers a part of the body

Smart Skills

Life skills

21ST CENTURY SKILLS

Visit a veterinary clinic, meet the doctor and find out the following:

- What should you do when you come across a lost puppy or a kitten?
- What kind of regular medical check-up is required for domestic animals?

Sense of hearing

Animals use their ears to hear. However, not all have visible ears.

Snakes don't have external ears and can feel the sound vibrations from the ground. They cannot hear the flute being played by the snake charmer. Similarly, fish have internal ears that sense sound vibrations in water.

An elephant hears with the help of its feet when sound travels through the ground. Bats are blind but they fly and hunt with the help of their sense of hearing. They produce **high-pitched** sounds. The **echo** of these sounds helps them locate food or sense danger. Similarly, whales and dolphins produce different sounds like clicks and whistles and use the echo of these sounds to move through water.

Dolphins

Sense of touch

The sense of touch is distributed throughout the body through our skin and hair. When we touch something, nerve endings in our skin pass that information to the brain, which in turn tells us what we are feeling. The skin is the largest sense organ in the body. Hair on the skin magnifies the sensitivity and acts as an early warning system for the body.

Matter of Fact

Catfish are huge fish that do not have scales on their bodies. Their smooth skin gives them a sharp sense of touch. They have tiny hair on their bodies, which are sensitive to vibrations.

Cats have whiskers that are very sensitive to touch. They help cats find their way in the dark. Mice too have long whiskers that help them sense danger. The hair on the wings of butterflies helps them detect changes in air pressure.

high-pitched: a very loud sound; **echo:** a sound that is repeated in closed spaces

Give It a Shot

E

We know the world through our senses. They help us to enjoy our food, listen to music, think and understand. Imagine if you had to live one day without one of your senses.

- List the things you would not be able to do without that sense.
- Which sense you felt was very important and which was least? Why?

How Animals Communicate

Animals communicate with each other and with people around them in many interesting ways. The sense organs of animals help them communicate with each other through sounds, smells and touch. Dogs communicate their feelings of joy, anger or fear by barking and growling. Monkeys howl to send warning signs about an **oncoming** danger. Honeybees tell each other where to find nectar or where to build a hive by flying in a special way. These movements are called the **bee dance**.

How Animals Sleep

Bats

All animals get tired and need to rest and sleep, like humans, but they do not do it in the same way as we do. Some animals need more sleep than us. Tigers need sixteen hours of sleep per day. A koala bear spends eighteen hours of the day sleeping and the rest of the time eating bamboo leaves. Some animals hardly sleep at all. Giraffes sleep for only twenty minutes in a day. Animals sleep differently too. Horses sleep while standing and cows sleep with eyes open. Dogs sleep with their eyes closed and bats sleep hanging upside down. Chimpanzees and gorillas like to curl up and sleep just like humans.

Smart Skills

Digital literacy

21ST CENTURY SKILLS

Click or collect pictures of five different animals or birds in and around your neighbourhood or your society. Find out for each: name of the animal and one interesting fact about the senses given below. Each group will make a PowerPoint presentation and present it to the class.

- Sense of smell
- Sense of sight
- Sense of touch
- Sense of taste
- Sense of hearing and communication

oncoming: approaching from the front

What We Learnt

Animal Senses

- **Sight**: Birds have powerful eyesight because their eyes are bigger as compared to the size of their heads.
- **Hearing**: Snakes and fish hear with the help of sound vibrations.
- **Smell**: In dogs and ants sense of smell is well developed.
- **Touch**: Whiskers of cats and mice help them to find their way in the dark and sense a predator.
- **Taste**: Butterflies, bees and houseflies taste with their feet.
- Animals communicate with each other but not like human beings.
- Different animals sleep for different time periods and in different ways.

Think and Answer

A. Fill in the blanks with the correct answers.

1. The Jacobson's Organ is the sensory organ of a ....
   a. snake b. bee c. dog
2. Many bats find their way by listening to ....
   a. music b. the sound of animals c. an echo
3. The taste buds of butterflies are on their ....
   a. tongue b. feet c. wings
4. A .... uses whiskers to detect things around it.
   a. bee b. shark c. cat
5. .... sleep with their eyes open.
   a. Horses b. Cows c. Dogs

B. Fill in the blanks.

1. Birds like .... and .... have powerful vision.
2. Some animals like .... produce high-pitched sounds.

3. .... sleep standing, while.. like to curl up and sleep.
4. Ants use their .... to find their way and to ....
5. Flies and mosquitoes have .... eyes.

C. Write *T* for true and *F* for false.

1. Elephants hear with the help of their feet. ☐
2. Skin is the largest sense organ in our body. ☐
3. Snakes smell with the help of their nose. ☐
4. Human beings have a strong sense of smell, which is stronger than that of a dog. ☐
5. Giraffes sleep only for twenty hours a day. ☐

D. Answer these questions.

1. Why do animals need sense organs?
2. What are antennae and how are they used?
3. Why do butterflies walk on leaves before laying their eggs?
4. How do snakes smell and taste?
5. How do animals communicate with other animals and human beings?

Cross Connect

HC CC

Listen and Draw Activity

Materials Needed: Pictures, drawing sheet and colours

Form pairs and sit back-to-back with your partner close enough to talk and listen to each other. Your teacher will give your partner a picture, and a drawing sheet and colours to you. You cannot look at the picture, but your partner will describe it very clearly to you. Draw the picture as described by your partner. You may ask questions to your partner. Once done, compare the original picture with your drawing. You may use different languages during the activity but only one at a time.

Web link

For more information, log on to:
https://www.nationalgeographic.com/animals/article/141122-crabs-snakes-smell-taste-nose-science-biology

Last accessed on 30 August 2021

6. Our Forests

Unit 2: Plants and Animals

Get Going

Endangered Wildlife

Our wildlife is endangered, as animals like the tiger, elephant, rhino, leopard, lizard and many snake species have been hunted for sports since ages. The illegal wildlife trade is being driven by demand for products made from various animal parts such as tusks of elephants and rhinos and skin of tigers and leopards. Many birds are also being **poached** in many parts of the country. In order to control poaching, the government has declared many areas as wildlife sanctuaries, bird sanctuaries and national parks. Wildlife is our heritage, and it is our duty to preserve every species of animal for the future generations. It is important for us to conserve both the forests as well as its wildlife.

- What would you do to conserve forest and wildlife?

Forests are large areas where many trees grow. They are found in many places around the world.

Importance of Forests

- Forests release a large amount of oxygen in the environment and absorb carbon dioxide from it. Therefore, they clean the air.
- Forests are natural habitats for birds, animals and insects.
- Forests prevent soil **erosion** caused by heavy rainfall. The roots of the trees help to hold the soil in place.
- Leaves that fall off the trees form a protective layer on the soil, which allows water to seep into the soil and refill the groundwater. They also prevent **landslides** and floods.

Matter of Fact

Padma Shri Jadav Payeng from Majuli is known as the Forest Man of India. He planted trees on a small piece of land on the banks of the Brahmaputra in Jorhat. This piece of land is now a forest and is known as Molai Forest.

poach: to illegally hunt birds, animals or fish on somebody else's property or without permission; **erosion:** slow removal of soil from the ground; **landslides:** when a piece of land breaks off from a mountain or a cliff

- Forests are a source of food and natural resources. They are also a source of **livelihood** for many people.
- Forests help in increasing rainfall and keeping the climate cool in a region.
- Forests act as **barriers** to strong winds and protect the regions around them from storms.
- Forests absorb sound and act as natural barriers for unwanted noise.
- Forests are a rich source of medicines.

Picture Study

- Have you ever visited a forest? Name the forest.
- How is it different from where you live?

People Living in the Forests

Human beings lived in jungles before cities and towns developed. They lived in small groups called **tribes**. People who live in tribes are called **tribal people**. As towns and cities developed, many of these people started moving out of the forests. The clearing of forests by cutting down trees also forced them to move to cities. However, a large population of these people continues to live in forests till today.

Tribes of India

Different states of India have different tribes, each having a unique culture, language, clothing and lifestyle.

- The Bhils live in Madhya Pradesh, Maharashtra, Gujarat and Rajasthan. This community is famous for its Gair dance and Pithora painting.
- The Gondi people or Gonds live in Madhya Pradesh, Chhattisgarh, Maharashtra, Telangana, Andra Pradesh, Bihar and Odisha.
- The Santhal people or Santhals live in Jharkhand, West Bengal, Bihar, Odisha and Assam.
- Some of the tribes of the northeastern states of India are Garo, Khasi, Jaintia, Bhutia, Kuki and Bodo.

Indian tribesman

livelihood: source of money or food; **barrier:** a fence or other obstacle that prevents movement or access

- The Great Andamanese, Onge, Jarawa and Sentinelese are tribes of the Andaman and Nicobar Islands.
- The Irula is a tribe of south India. They inhabit parts of Tamil Nadu, Karnataka, Andhra Pradesh and Kerala. The Irula people are expert snake and rat catchers and that is what makes them special. They are largely dependent on agricultural products such as paddy, ragi and dal.

Jarawa people

- The Chenchu tribes inhabit the forests of the Nallamala Hills in Andhra Pradesh and Telangana. The Chenchu people are dependent on hunting and trading jungle products, such as roots, fruits, tubers, tendu leaves, mahua flower and honey. They speak a language that closely resembles Telugu.

Social and economic life

People who live in forests depend on it for food and shelter. They are engaged in various occupations, like agriculture primarily shifting cultivation (jhum), hunting, gathering and fishing. Handicrafts that are made from forest products like bamboo, leaves and lac are traditional art forms practiced by many tribes of India.

Mats, leaf plates, baskets, ropes, jewellery and decorative items are some examples of handicrafts. Weaving is another important occupation, resulting in many distinct patterns, each native to specific regions or tribes. Tribes have a distinct music and dance that are common during religious and agricultural festivals. Religion is of great importance to the people and most of the tribes perform **elaborate rituals** during festivals or religious ceremonies. Many associate God with nature, hence, they worship natural forces like the Sun, rain, or fire. Each tribe engages in a variety of traditional games and sports as a form of recreation. Today, old habits and customs live on and continue to be practised alongside development in many tribal societies.

Santhal women

Skilling Up

Information literacy

21ST CENTURY SKILLS

- What are scheduled tribes?
- On an outline political map of India, write down the names of two tribes from each state.
- Are there any states in India that do not have any tribal population?

elaborate: detailed or complicated; **ritual:** a religious ceremony

Deforestation

The cutting down of trees on a large scale is called **deforestation**. It involves a complete and long-term removal of tree cover without planting trees back. Deforestation is one of the biggest threats to the tribal people who live in forests.

Causes of deforestation

Agriculture: The forest cover of a region is often removed to convert it into agricultural land which is used for growing crops to meet the food requirement of the people.

Increase in population: An increase in population leads to an increased demand for land, roads and houses. To meet these demands, forests are being cut down at a very fast rate.

Overgrazing: Exposing a region to cattle grazing for a long period removes the plant and grass cover of the region.

Commercial activity: The cutting of trees for firewood and building materials is a major cause of deforestation.

Smart Skills — Communication — 21ST CENTURY SKILLS

13 CLIMATE ACTION

- Forest fires are wildfires where an uncontrolled fire rages through vegetation generally more than six feet in height. Wildfires are caused either naturally by friction of falling stones, dryness, animal activities, by lightening or by human actions. Discuss in class.
- In recent times have you heard of forest fires in any part of the world?
- Find out their causes and effects.

Forest fires: Natural and man-made fires often destroy forests.

Effects of deforestation

- Deforestation causes natural disasters such as floods and droughts.
- It leads to soil erosion as the land loses its plant cover.
- Deforestation can cause an increase in desert area.
- Air pollution increases when many trees are cut.
- Deforestation endangers the lives of wild animals and the tribal people, as it destroys their natural habitat.
- It causes unexpected **climate change** in a region.

Deforestation in Tawang, Arunachal Pradesh

climate change: a change in climate, generally a rise or fall in the normal temperature of a place, caused because of pollution

Conservation of Forests

To protect, to save or preserve is known as **conservation**. We are dependent on forests for many things. By destroying them, we are causing an imbalance in nature. It is important that we conserve trees and plants that we still have.

Role of the government

Forest conservation is a worldwide concern. The destruction of forests causes an imbalance between humans and nature. Conservation of forest resources can be done by joint efforts of the government, non-government organisations and the public through a proper management system.

Give It a Shot E

15 LIFE ON LAND

Biosphere reserves are the areas used to conserve plants, animals, and microorganisms. It covers a large area of land and contains many wildlife sanctuaries and national parks.

- How many biosphere reserves are there in India?
- Write names of five biosphere reserves of India.

India is home to a wide variety of animals like tigers, elephants, rhinoceroses, leopards, lizards and many species of snakes.

To protect wildlife, national parks and wildlife sanctuaries have been set up in different parts of the country. A **national park** is a reserved area where wild animals can roam freely, and the threats of hunting and poaching are illegal.

Sanctuaries are places where animals are given freedom to live in their natural surroundings safely and are protected throughout their lives.

India is home to 70 percent of tigers in the world. The **Project Tiger** was launched in 1973, to maintain the population of tigers in their natural habitats and to protect them from extinction. The Jim Corbett National Park in Uttarakhand and the Kaziranga National Park in Assam are some examples.

Jim Corbett National Park

Smart Skills — Digital literacy (21st Century Skills)

In groups of four, select two national parks or wildlife sanctuaries of India. Find out the names of five animals, birds and trees found there. Make a short power point presentation.

Role of the people

The local population of the area works for conservation of the forested area.

Sacred groves: Protecting trees in sacred **groves** is a traditional method of forest conservation. In many cultures, **tracts** of forests are set aside and all the trees and wildlife within are worshipped and are fully protected. These tracts are called **sacred groves** and are known by different local names throughout the country. Himachal Pradesh has the maximum number of sacred groves in the country.

Mawphlang sacred groves in Meghalaya

Chipko Movement: The Chipko Movement, also called the **Chipko Andolan**, was a **non-violent** movement that originated in Uttarakhand in the 1970s. The movement was a protest to the large-scale destruction of forests in the Garhwal region of the Himalayas. The Hindi word *chipko* means 'to hug' or 'to cling'. Men and women living in the forests participated in the movement by embracing trees and saving them from being axed.

The tree-huggers: The Bishnoi people are a group of tribal people from Rajasthan and northern India. The Bishnois are known to have sacrificed their lives for saving trees. Amrita Devi was a young Bishnoi girl who sacrificed her life to save trees in Khejarli, a village in Jodhpur. When she learnt that the soldiers sent by the ruler of Jodhpur were ordered to cut the trees of the village for firewood, she hugged the trees to prevent them from being cut. However, the soldiers did not stop, and Amrita lost her life. The sacrifice she made, encouraged others in her village who started hugging the trees to save them. It is said that nearly 363 Bishnoi people lost their lives during this movement. This earned the Bishnoi tribe the title of tree-huggers.

Smart Skills — Life skills — 21ST CENTURY SKILLS

What role will you play in protecting the environment?

Van Mahotsav: Van Mahotsav is a 7-day festival celebrated annually in India. It is organized every year in July. During this festival, many trees are planted by people across the country. Van Mahotsav means the festival of forests. This festival was started in 1950 by Kanaiyalal Maneklal Munshi, who was a famous **environmentalist** and the Minister of Agriculture and Food during that time. People participate in this festival by planting saplings in their homes, schools, colleges and offices.

tract: an area of land, especially a large one; **grove:** a group of trees that are close together; **non-violent:** using peaceful means or methods; **environmentalist:** a person who is concerned about protecting the environment

What We Learnt

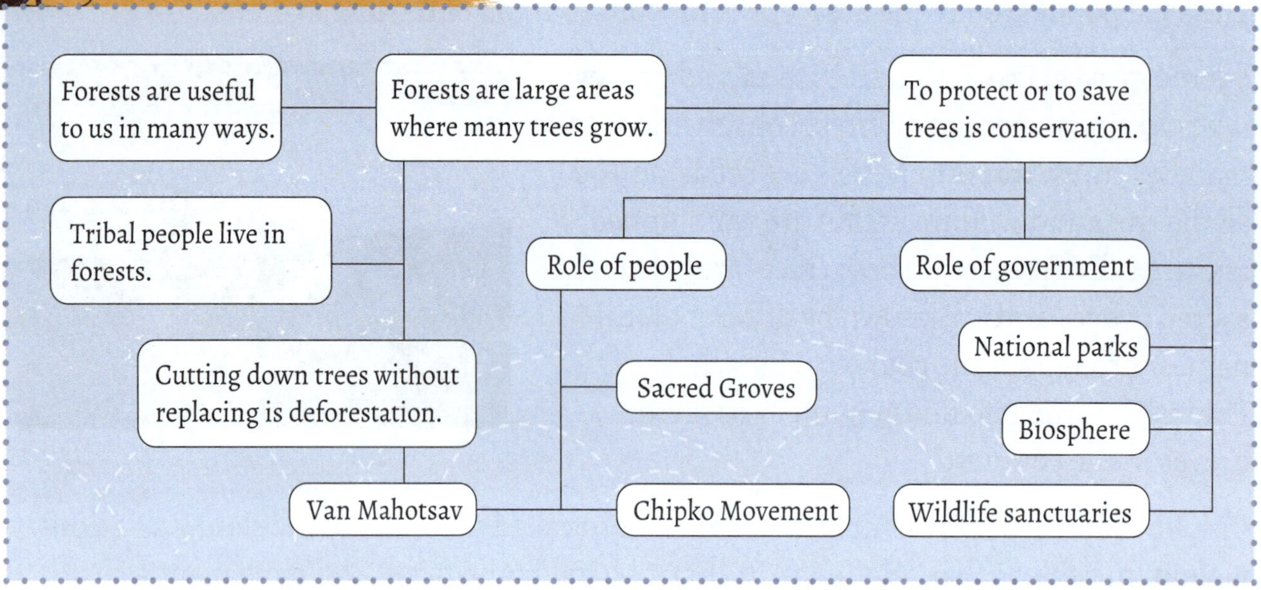

Think and Answer

A. Fill in the blanks.

1. .... are important natural resources.
2. Forests prevent soil .... caused by heavy rainfall.
3. The .... are the largest tribal groups in India.
4. The Bhil community is famous for .... painting.
5. The Chipko Movement originated in the state of ....

B. Fill in the blanks with the correct answers.

1. The Hindi word chipko means ....
   a. to cut b. to cling c. to plant d. to celebrate
2. The Chenchu are the tribal people of ....
   a. Gujarat b. Manipur c. Andhra Pradesh d. Jharkhand
3. The .... are tribal people from the Andaman and Nicobar Islands.
   a. Garo b. Khasi c. Jarawa d. Gonds
4. Van Mahotsav was started in ....
   a. 1970 b. 1978 c. 1988 d. 1950
5. The Project Tiger was launched to protect tigers from ....
   a. destruction b. extinction c. operation d. affection

C. Write *T* for true and *F* for false.

1. The Bishnoi people are also called tree-huggers. ☐
2. Overgrazing poses a threat to many kinds of plant species. ☐
3. Himachal Pradesh has the maximum number of sacred groves in the world. ☐
4. The Chipko Movement started In India in 1965. ☐
5. Van Mahotsav is a two-day festival. ☐

D. Answer these questions.

1. Why are forests important?
2. Why and when was the Project Tiger launched?
3. Write a short paragraph on the tribal people of India.
4. What are sacred groves?
5. What is the Chipko Movement? How did people try to save trees during this movement?

Cross Connect

Leaf-stamped Bookmarks

Collect different types of fallen leaves. Take papers, and paints and a paintbrush. Apply a generous amount of paint to the back of your leaf. Press firmly on the paper, and press each part so that the leaf veins make a beautiful impression. Use this to make gift wraps, cards and bookmarks.

Web link

For more information, log on to:
https://www.nationalgeographic.com/travel/article/partner-content-india-wildlife-places

Last accessed on 30 August 2021

7. Aquatic Life

Unit 2: Plants and Animals

Get Going

Aquatic Weeds

Plants that grow rapidly and often cover the surface of water bodies, thus preventing sunlight from reaching the plants underwater are known as aquatic weeds. Too many weeds can block access to the water make it difficult by reducing oxygen levels and nutrients in the water that are essential for fish to **thrive**.

Sea kelp

These weeds are major cause of pollution and foul smell in water bodies. Therefore, it is necessary to check and control their growth. Kelp are seaweeds that grow in as underwater forests. They are found in oceans throughout the world.

- Have you seen aquatic weeds? Where?

Aquatic Plants

Plants that are **adapted** to live in water are called **aquatic plants**. They are found in seas, oceans, rivers, streams, lakes and ponds. Aquatic plants are of four types—**free-floating plants**, **rooted-floating plants**, **submerged plants** and **emergent plants**.

Free-floating plants

Plants that float freely in water or on the surface of water are called **free-floating plants**. The presence of spongy, air-filled parts makes them light and helps them float easily. Their roots are not fixed to the soil and can absorb all nutrients from the water. They also provide shade to animals living in water. Duckweed, *Pistia* or water lettuce and water hyacinth are free-floating plants. Water hyacinth has thick, oval-shaped leaves that help it to float in water. It also has long and spongy stalks and feather-like roots. Water fern has many scale-like leaves that help it to float.

Duckweed

thrive: to grow strongly and vigorously; **adapted:** behaviour changed in order to survive in new environments

Rooted-floating plants

The roots of some plants are fixed in the soil but their leaves float on the surface of water. The stems are hollow and **supple**, which help them move with the **water current** and protect the plant from damage. Their leaves are flat and broad. Lotuses and water lilies are examples of **rooted-floating plants.**

Lotus

Picture Study

How are aquatic plants different from plants found on land?

Skilling Up

Critical thinking — 21ST CENTURY SKILLS

How would you remove aquatic weeds without causing harm to aquatic life? What will happen to aquatic life if it is left to grow? Why?

Submerged plants

Submerged plants grow under water and their roots are fixed in the soil. They have narrow, needle-like leaves that allow the water currents to flow through them without causing any damage. They absorb carbon dioxide and keep the water clean. Tape grass or *Vallisneria*, *Hydrilla* and eelgrass are submerged plants.

Emergent plants

Emergent aquatic plants grow along the banks of ponds or lakes, or in **shallow** and **marshy** areas. They have long narrow leaves that extend out of the water, while the lower part of these plants remains under water. The narrow leaves help them bend easily and prevent them from breaking when there is strong wind or waves. Bulrush and arum lily are emergent plants.

Bulrush

supple: something that bends and moves easily; **water current:** speed of moving water; **shallow:** of little depth; **marshy:** soft and wet

Smart Skills

Digital literacy

21ST CENTURY SKILLS

Form two groups and make a short PowerPoint presentation to address these questions:

- How does water pollution affect aquatic life?
- What would your role be in saving aquatic life?

14 LIFE BELOW WATER

Give It a Shot

E

Find one difference between rooted floating plants, submerged plants and emergent plants. Give one example each in the table given below.

Rooted floating plants	Submerged plants	Emergent plants

Aquatic Animals

Animals that live in or on the surface of water bodies are called **aquatic animals**. Aquatic animals that live in freshwater bodies, such as rivers, lakes and streams, are called **freshwater animals**. Aquatic animals that live in saltwater bodies, such as oceans and seas, are called **marine animals**.

Sea lion

Some aquatic animals, such as fish, octopuses and seahorses live in water throughout their life. Animals such as walruses, tortoises and sea lions live in water but come to land to **breed** and to take rest. They are called **semi-aquatic animals**. Animals such as newts, salamanders and frogs live both in water and on land, but they lay their eggs in water. They are called **amphibians**. Snails and starfish are found deep in water, whereas dragonflies and pond skaters are found on the surface of water. Flamingos and ducks live near water.

Starfish

breed: to reproduce

Adaptations in aquatic animals

Fish have a streamlined body that is broad at the centre and **tapers** towards the ends. They have fins that are used for balancing and **steering** through the water. The tail fin is used to move forward and the scales, which are bony, protect the soft bodies of the fish. They breathe in water through **gills**.

Animals with shells, such as sea turtles, crabs and lobsters, breathe through their gills. The limbs of sea turtles are like **flippers**, which are adapted for swimming. The forelimbs are long and paddle-like and the hindlimbs act as **rudders**. Lobsters curl and uncurl their abdomens to swim.

Matter of Fact

The **Atlantic wolfish** are sometimes called wolf eels because of their long bodies.

They are not aggressive towards people, despite their scary look.

Lobster

Ducks have webbed feet that help them swim in water. Ducks do not have nerves or blood vessels in their feet. Therefore, they do not feel cold even if they swim in cold water. Their feathers are waterproof and a special gland that produces oil is located near the tail.

Some birds like flamingos have long legs that help them **wade** in water, thus keeping their bodies dry. Their long necks help them reach below the water for food.

Smart Skills

Information literacy

21ST CENTURY SKILLS

Life under water is different from the one outside it.

- What are special features of frogs that live on land as well as in water.
- Crocodiles live mostly in water. How are they able to live on the land?

Frogs and toads are amphibians. Their skin helps them breathe when they are in water, while their lungs help them to breathe on land. They have webbed feet that help them swim.

Aquatic mammals, such as whales and dolphins, breathe through their lungs. They keep coming up to the water surface to breathe.

taper: to become gradually narrower; **steering:** moving something in a certain direction; **gill:** an organ through which fish and other water creatures breathe; **flippers:** body parts of some sea animals that help them to swim; **rudder:** a part of an object that controls its movement; **wade:** walking through water

Stagnant Water

Stagnant water and the organisms living in it cause diseases. Stagnant water is found in ponds, lakes, pools, tanks, water coolers, puddles and outdoor places where water gets collected.

Mosquitoes and diseases

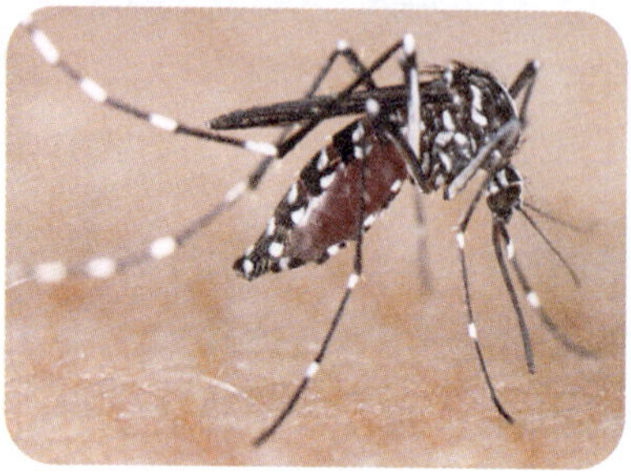

Aedes aegypti

Some aquatic animals like certain insects that live in freshwater and dirty water are harmful to us as they cause diseases. Mosquitoes feed on the blood of humans and animals. They are not aquatic animals, but they lay eggs in **stagnant** or slow-moving water. The eggs of a mosquito hatch within 24 to 48 hours of laying. The newly hatched mosquitoes or **larvae** reach the pupa stage in 7 to 10 days, and then turn into mosquitoes. Female mosquitoes lay up to 100 eggs at a time. Dengue, chikungunya and yellow fever are spread by the *Aedes aegypti* mosquito that breeds in both clean and stagnant water.

Malaria is caused by a **parasite** called **plasmodium** that lives inside the body of a mosquito. The mosquito picks up the parasite by biting an already infected person. When the mosquito carrying the parasite bites a healthy person, it injects the parasite into the person's blood, thus causing malaria. The female anopheles mosquito acts as a carrier for the disease.

Symptoms and diagnosis

Diagnosis is the identification of a disease. To diagnose malaria, chikungunya or dengue, a blood test is carried out.

Symptoms		
Malaria	**Dengue**	**Chikungunya**
• High fever • Severe headache • Chills • Vomiting and **convulsions**	• High fever • Severe headache • Muscle ache • Joint pain and rashes • Vomiting and **nausea**	• High fever and chills • Pain in the abdomen, eyes, joints and muscles • Headache • Skin rash

A person showing such symptoms must be taken to a doctor. A medicine from the **cinchona** plant, known as **quinine**, is used to treat malaria. Malaria may be treated with anti-malarial drugs, which can be given orally or through an injection.

stagnant: not moving; **larvae:** a baby insect; **parasite:** a living thing that lives on or inside another living thing and gets its food from it; **convulsions:** a sudden violent movement of body; **nausea:** a feeling of sickness

Prevention and control

The following preventive measures can control the spread of diseases caused by mosquitoes:

- Wear clothes that cover your entire body while sleeping.
- Wire screens on windows prevent mosquitoes from entering the house. Use a mosquito net while sleeping.
- Apply chemical or oil-based mosquito **repellents** to protect yourself from mosquito bites.
- Eliminate any stagnant water sources in or around the neighbourhood with the help of municipality workers.
- Old tyres, buckets, ceramic pots and other containers that collect rain water should be disposed of.
- Empty stagnant water from water coolers or add kerosene oil at least once a week to prevent the breeding of mosquitoes.
- In emergency situations, local health authorities may carry out **fogging** or spraying to kill mosquitoes breeding in an area.
- We must keep our surroundings clean to avoid diseases caused by mosquitoes.

Smart Skills — Life skills — 21st Century Skills

What are the ways to prevent ourselves from contracting malaria and dengue?

What We Learnt

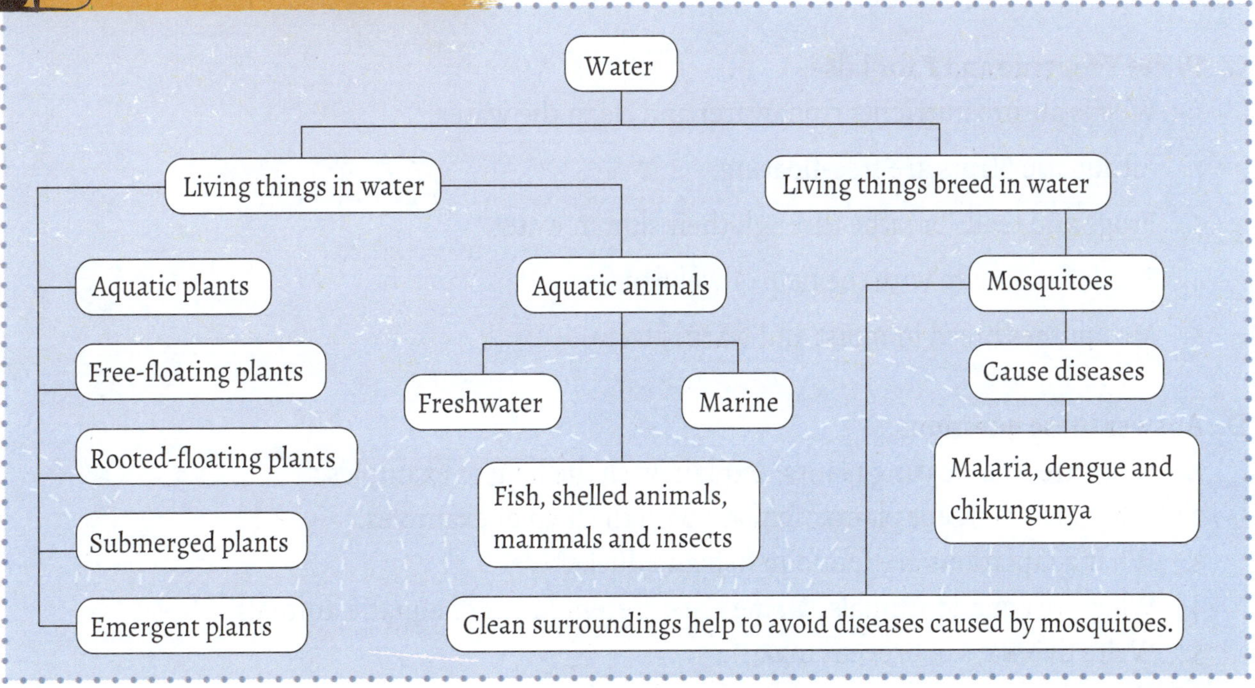

repellent: a substance that drives away insects; **fogging:** the act of spraying a place with chemicals that kills harmful insects

Think and Answer

A. Fill in the blanks with the correct answers.

1. .... is a free-floating plant.
   a. Duckweed b. Water lily c. Hydrilla d. Bulrush
2. Submerged plants have .... roots.
   a. air-filled b. flat and broad c. needle-like d. long and narrow
3. .... curl and uncurl their abdomens to swim.
   a. Crabs b. Lobsters c. Whales d. Sea turtles
4. A medicine, known as quinine from the plant ...., is used to treat malaria.
   a. cardamom b. cinchona c. cinnamon d. chinar
5. The female anopheles mosquito causes ....
   a. malaria b. dengue c. chikungunya d. yellow fever

B. Write two examples of each.

1. Submerged plants ...., ...
2. Free-floating plants ...., ...
3. Diseases caused by mosquitoes ...., ...
4. Animals that breathe through gills ...., ...
5. Amphibians ...., ...

C. Write *T* for true and *F* for false.

1. Weeds absorb nutrients from water and clean the water. ☐
2. All aquatic plants are free-floating. ☐
3. Frogs and toads breathe through their skin in water. ☐
4. Turtles can swim with the help of webbed feet. ☐
5. Mosquitoes breed in moist and warm places. ☐

D. Answer these questions.

1. What are free-floating plants? Explain with the help of examples.
2. What are emergent plants? Explain with the help of examples.
3. What adaptations are found in fish and ducks?
4. What are aquatic animals? Name the different kinds of aquatic animals.
5. Write five ways to prevent malaria.
6. How can we prevent mosquitoes from breeding?

Cross Connect

Make a Diorama

Let us make a diorama of an aquarium. A diorama is a model that represents a scene in three dimensions.

Things needed: A shoe box, transparent plastic sheet, coloured paper, paints, scissors, craft knife, glue, tape, stapler, crayons, markers and thread.

Paint the inside of the shoe box in shades of blue so that it looks like the ocean. Paint or draw with crayons, plants in water. Using the coloured paper, cut out shapes of different aquatic animals, like crabs, fish, whales and dolphins. Make holes in the cut outs and using the thread, hang the cut outs inside the box from the top. Cover the face of the box with the plastic sheet. Display your diorama in class.

Web link

For more information, log on to:
https://kids.nationalgeographic.com/pages/topic/ocean-portal

Last accessed on 30 August 2021

8. Be Wise and Healthy

Unit 3: Work and Play

Get Going

Dutee's Story

Many people in the past used to think that women should not participate in sports. They were discouraged from taking part in sports all over the world and especially in India where it was believed that girls should only do housework. However, over the years there have been major changes in participation of women in sports. Let us read about Dutee Chand, the only Indian woman athlete to have qualified for the 100 metres race in the Olympics.

Dutee Chand

Dutee was born to weaver parents in Odisha. She was inspired to take up running by her older sister. Not being able to afford the shoes to practise, she would run barefoot around the lake. Several people would tell her that this is not something a girl should be doing. Today she is an international sportsperson. 'It has been a long, hard journey. People now see me for my sport and my hard work', says Dutee.

- Where do you go to play?
- What games do you play?
- Have you ever been stopped from playing? Why?

Playing games is a recreational activity done in leisure time for fun. Games are played for entertainment or exercise. Games are also played for achievement and rewards. They are played individually or in teams by **amateurs** or **professionals**. In many games, people play against other people. Playing games keeps us fit and helps us maintain a healthy mind, body and soul. We learn many values while playing games just as we learn to take defeat in the right spirit.

amateurs: people who take part in a sport or other activities for enjoyment, not as a job; **professional:** connected with a job that needs special training or skill

Games and sports are played by following a set of rules. However, they are different from each other. Games played for a competition or professionally for a reward is a sport. Games are played for enjoyment and relaxation. The difference lies in the purpose of playing. People who play games are called players while those who play a sport are called sportspersons. Games can be played by both amateurs or professionals.

Give It a Shot

E

Tic-Tac-Toe

In pairs, play Tic-Tac-Toe with your partner in these grids. Your objective is to get three X's in a row before your partner gets three O's in a row.

Types of Games

Games are of two types—**indoor games** and **outdoor games**. These can be further divided as **individual games** and **team games**.

Individual games

In individual games or sports, participants play individually. A single player competes with another single player. He or she performs according to the skills they need to achieve their goal. Cycling, swimming, golf, shooting, archery and javelin throw are some individual games. Neeraj Chopra, an Indian athlete won a gold medal for men's javelin throw at the **2020 Tokyo Olympics**.

Neeraj Chopra

Team games

In team games or sports, two or more players play against a team of players of the same number. The objective is to win the game together as a team. Team games are played according to a set of rules. **Referees** or **umpires** are people who ensure that the rules are followed. Basketball, cricket, kabaddi, hockey and football are some team games.

Basketball

Picture Study

In a football match the referee is seen running with the players and making some signs with his or her hands and body. Look at the pictures and write what the signal means below each picture.

1. ....

2. ....

3. ....

4. ....

5. ....

6. ....

Team Spirit

Striving to achieve a common goal together is known as **team spirit**. It can also be defined as playing with unity to win a game. Friendship and trust amongst the players of a team are important for team spirit. All members of a team are important, irrespective of whether they are girls or boys or their state, region, religion or economic background.

Team spirit

striving: to try very hard to achieve something

Important aspects of team spirit

Some important aspects of team spirit are:

- A game is played for the team and not for ourselves.
- The common aim of a team is enjoying and winning the game against the opponent.
- The players of a team respect each other.
- Each player of a team has the right to present their opinions.
- All the players of a team follow team discipline.

Smart Skills — Life skills (21st Century Skills)

Imagine that you have been made the captain of your section's sports team for the upcoming inter section sports competitions. How will you bring team spirit and trust in your team so that you can win the competition?

The leader of a team is called a **captain**. To be a good captain, one should be caring, courageous and dependable. He or she should listen to the teammates and encourage and respect them. A captain is also the **mentor** of the teammates. Captains plan and discuss **strategies** with their teammates. All team members should trust and respect the captain. Can you name some successful sports captains of India?

Smart Skills — Problem-solving (21st Century Skills)

Have you been part of your class team for sports, choir, dance or theatre? If so, which team? What was your role in the team? What are some of the values you learnt as part of the team? What were some of the difficulties you faced? How did you overcome them? Discuss this during **circle time** with your teacher and class.

Playing Together

Boys and girls often play together as a mixed team when playing in the park or in their neighbourhood for games such as seven tiles or *pitthu*, hide-and-seek and *kho kho*. In competitive or national level sports, boys and girls play in separate teams. Men and women represent India in sports like hockey, football, basketball and cricket in separate men's and women's teams. Lawn tennis, table tennis and badminton are some competitive sports that are played both in separate as well as mixed teams.

Both girls and boys should be allowed to follow their passion for sports and games even after completing their education. In recent times, the outlook towards participation of girls in games and sports has started to change. Women are encouraged to participate

mentor: an experienced person who advises and helps somebody with less experience over a period; **strategies:** a plan that is intended to achieve a purpose; **accolade:** praise or an award for an achievement

in both. Thus, they have started to bring **accolades** for their country. India's women's cricket and hockey teams have made a name for themselves. At the 2020 Tokyo Olympics female sportspersons from India won big. Mirabai Chanu won silver medal in women's 49kg weightlifting. Lovlina Borgohain and P.V. Sindhu won bronze medals in women's welterweight boxing and women's singles badminton.

These are some Indian female sportspersons who have reached the top against all odds.

Mirabai Chanu

Lovlina Borgohain

P.V. Sindhu

Can you name some more female sportspersons from India?

National Teams

Mahendra Singh Dhoni

Teams that represent a country in a competitive sport are called **national teams**. Sportspersons who play in national teams are called **national level players**. Some of the famous national level players from India are Mahendra Singh Dhoni, Virat Kohli, Saina Nehwal and Sania Mirza. The Indian men's hockey team won a bronze medal at the 2020 Tokyo Olympics.

Traditional Games of India

Games that have been played in India since ancient times are called **traditional games**. They are played using minimum equipment.

Kho kho is a game that was first played by the people of Maharashtra. It is also known as a 'game of chase'. The word *kho* is derived from Sanskrit and means 'get up and go'. This game is played between two teams of nine players each. **Boat race**, or *Vallam Kali*, is the traditional boat race of Kerala. It is organised during the harvest festival, Onam. Paddled war canoes are used during the race. **Gilli danda** is a game played with two sticks.

Matter of Fact

Pachisi is a boardgame that was quite popular in ancient India. The game is mentioned in the epic *Mahabharata* as *Chausar*. Emperor Akbar and his descendants also played this game. Ludo, which you must have played, originated from Pachisi or Chausar.

accolade: praise or an award for an achievement

The larger stick is called *danda* and the smaller one *gilli*. This game is known by various names in India. The player strikes the gilli, which is balanced on a stone, so that it flips into the air. While it is in the air, the player runs to touch a point outside the circle before the gilli is caught by the opponent. **Kabaddi**, kite flying, dog and bone, marbles or *kancha* and hopscotch or *stapoo* are some other traditional games played in India.

Martial Arts

Martial arts are a form of sports practised for self-defence and fitness. Boxing, karate, taekwondo, judo, kung fu and wrestling are some types of martial arts. Ravi Kumar Dahiya and Bajrang Punia are Indian wrestlers who won silver and bronze medals at the 2020 Tokyo Olympics. There are many different types of martial arts. These forms had their origin in different parts of Asia, Europe and Africa.

Ravi Kumar Dahiya

There are some forms of martial arts that are traditional to India. **Kushti** is a form of wrestling. In this game, the wrestler or *pehlwan* learns how to fight from his guru or *ustad*. Some of the other martial art forms that originated in India are *Thang-ta* from Manipur, *Musti-yuddha* from Varanasi, *Gatka* from Punjab, *Silambam* from Tamil Nadu and *Kalaripayattu* from Kerala.

Kalaripayattu

Skilling Up

Information literacy

21ST CENTURY SKILLS

The coloured belt system in the martial arts was created by Dr Kano Jigoro of Japan. Just as you students receive certificates and medals, the belts were given as a reward. As the students improved and learned, the colour of their belts changed.

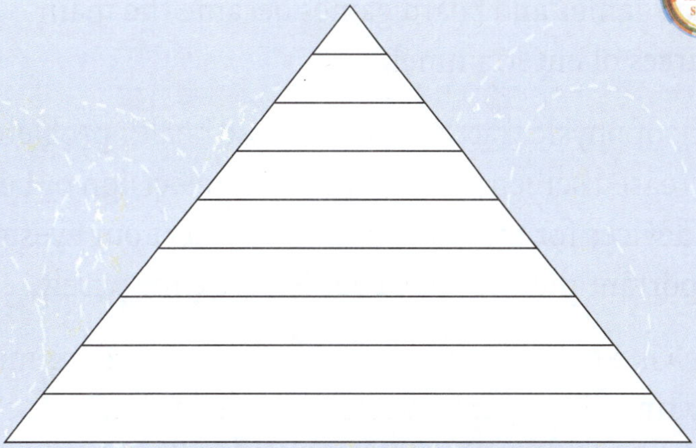

Colour the given pyramid in the correct order of the colours awarded to the students of martial arts starting with the first colour at the bottom of the pyramid with the final belt colour at the top.

Local games

Local games are games or sports that are popular in some region or state. Some local games of India are *Mallakhamba* from Maharashtra, wrestling from Haryana and *Thoda* from Himachal Pradesh. Which local game is played in your region?

Gymnastics

Acrobat

Gymnastics is a sport that requires balance, strength and flexibility. It is practised by both men and women. *Nats* are acrobats who perform gymnastics in Indian villages, cities and towns to entertain people. You must have seen children at traffic signals turning **cartwheels**, doing headstands and walking on tightropes. You may have seen men, women and children acrobats. *Nats* are also a nomadic tribe of India who move to different villages and cities performing acrobatics. They are very **agile** and their training starts from a very young age. Do you know the name of the first Indian gymnast in the Olympics? Did she win a medal? What is she famous for?

Leisure Time and Relaxation

Yoga

Relaxation is important for everyone. People relax in their leisure or free time by listening to music, reading books, watching television, playing board games or video games.

During the COVID- 19 lockdown, television, movies, video games and board games became the main sources of entertainment.

Lack of physical activities can cause health problems. Increased screen time by watching television or being on devices for too many hours can affect our eyesight and reduce concentration. It is important that we spend our leisure time wisely.

Yoga is a type of exercise that helps us relax our mind and can easily be done at home at any time. It prevents diseases and helps improve our concentration. We can be healthy and wise by participating actively in all kinds of games.

cartwheel: to turn over in the air; **agile:** able to move quickly and easily

What We Learnt

Playing games helps us maintain a healthy mind, body and soul. They increase our strength to fight diseases.

Games can be played indoors or outdoors, individually or in teams.

Sports are games played professionally or for a competition.

Games can played as a recreation for fun and excercise.

Martial arts are practiced for self-defence and fitness.

There are many traditional games of India. Gymnastics and martial arts too have been played since ancient times.

Friendship and trust amongst the players are important for team spirit.

Think and Answer

A. Fill in the blanks with the correct answers.

1. .... is also known as a 'game of chase'.
   a. Archery b. Kho kho c. Wrestling d. Cricket
2. Mary Kom represents India in ....
   a. hockey b. boxing c. wrestling d. football
3. Deepika Kumari represents India in ....
   a. archery b. shooting c. judo d. boxing
4. .... is played in mixed teams at the national level.
   a. Kho kho b. Cricket c. Tennis d. Football
5. .... is a type of martial art.
   a. Cartwheels b. Taekwondo c. Stapoo d. Gilli danda

B. Name the following.

1. Two individual games .... , ...
2. Two team games .... , ...
3. Two martial arts .... , ...
4. Two traditional games ...., ...
5. Two local games .... , ...

C. Write T for true and F for false.

1. In most professional sports, men and woman have separate teams.
2. The captain of a team has very little responsibility.
3. Schools should encourage boys and girls to play together.
4. Referees and umpires have a major role to play in sports.

D. Answer these questions.

1. Write names of four of your favourite players and the games they play.
2. How do you spend your leisure time?
3. Name three traditional games you play.
4. What is the difference between games and sports?
5. What are martial arts? Name three types.
6. Define team spirit.
7. What is the role of the captain of a team?

Cross Connect

Make a key holder

Repurpose your old things and make something useful.

Materials needed: Small old toys, rectangular plank of wood, hot glue gun, cloth hanger, hooks, paint

12 RESPONSIBLE CONSUMPTION AND PRODUCTION

Steps

1. Clean the old rectangular piece of wood.
2. Paste your old toys on it using the hot glue gun.
3. Paint the toys so that they look new and bright. You could use a single colour or many.
4. Paste the old cloth hanger on the back of the wooden piece using the hot glue gun.
5. Paste some hooks on the bottom edge of the wooden plank. This is where you can hang your keys.

Web link

For more information, log on to:
https://www.thebetterindia.com/10492/lesser-known-traditional-games-sports-india/

Last accessed on 30 August 2021

9. Breathe In, Breathe Out

Unit 3: Work and Play

Get Going

Look at the pictures and explain how would you use your breath.

....

List some more things where you use your breath.

All living things need water, food and air to live. We depend on air for our survival because it contains oxygen. Oxygen does not enter our bodies through the skin but through our mouths and noses. The process by which living things take in oxygen and breathe out carbon dioxide is called **breathing**. Taking in air through our nose or mouth into the lungs is called **inhalation**. Letting air out of lungs through nose is called **exhalation**.

Respiratory Organs

Respiration is the process by which oxygen absorbed during breathing is used by the body to break down food into energy. Breathing is a part of the respiratory process.

Many organs help us in respiration. They are mouth, nose, trachea, bronchi and lungs.

Matter of Fact

On an average adults breathe between 12 to 20 times a minute while resting. *Pranayama* is a practice of breath control. In Sanskrit *prana* is life energy and *yama* means control. It is the main component of yoga. It is a distinct breathing exercise and is usually practised after asanas.

Mouth and nose: We inhale or breathe in air through our nose or mouth. They warm, moisten and filter the incoming air. Tiny hair present inside the nostrils trap the dust particles present in the air.

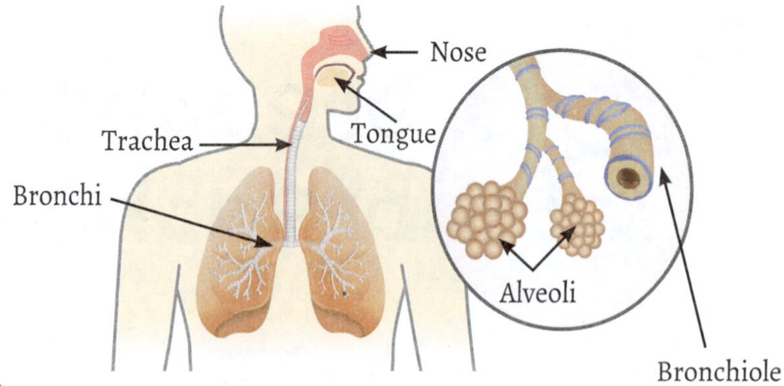

Human respiratory system

Trachea: The **trachea** or the **windpipe** allows the air to pass into the lungs through the mouth and nose. Tiny hair present in the inner membrane of the trachea, catch dust particles, which are removed by coughing.

Bronchi: The trachea branches out into two tubes called **bronchi**. Bronchi carry air into the lungs. They further branch into tiny tubes called **bronchioles**. **Alveoli** are found at the end of the bronchioles.

Lungs: These are one of the largest organs of the human body. They are a pair of spongy, air-filled organs located on either side of the chest. The human body has two lungs—the **right lung** and the **left lung**. The right lung is larger than the left lung. Lungs expand when we breathe in and contract when we breathe out.

The exchange of gases takes place in the lungs. Oxygen is absorbed and carbon dioxide is released. Oxygen absorbed by the lungs is supplied to all parts of the body through blood vessels.

The lungs are protected by a **ribcage**, which is made up of twelve sets of curved bones called ribs. These are connected to the spine and go around the lungs to keep them safe. The **diaphragm** is a strong muscle below the lungs. It controls breathing.

Smart Skills — Life skills — 21st Century Skills

We breathe out carbon dioxide which is a harmful gas. Too much of this gas is harmful to the environment.

- Suggest a simple step which will help in cleaning the environment.
- Make a poster of things we can do by blowing air.

How We Breathe

Our lungs expand when air is inhaled. The diaphragm moves down and creates space for the lungs. When we exhale air, the diaphragm relaxes and moves upward into the chest cavity, pushing the air out of the lungs.

The oxygen inhaled converts food we eat into energy during digestion. This energy is used up faster when we perform physical exercises like running, swimming and cycling. While doing such activities, our lungs absorb more oxygen and we breathe faster. When we require more oxygen, the heart also beats faster. Our breath becomes fast and deep so that our body gets more oxygen. The heartbeat can be heard by an instrument called **stethoscope**. It is used by the doctors to examine their patients.

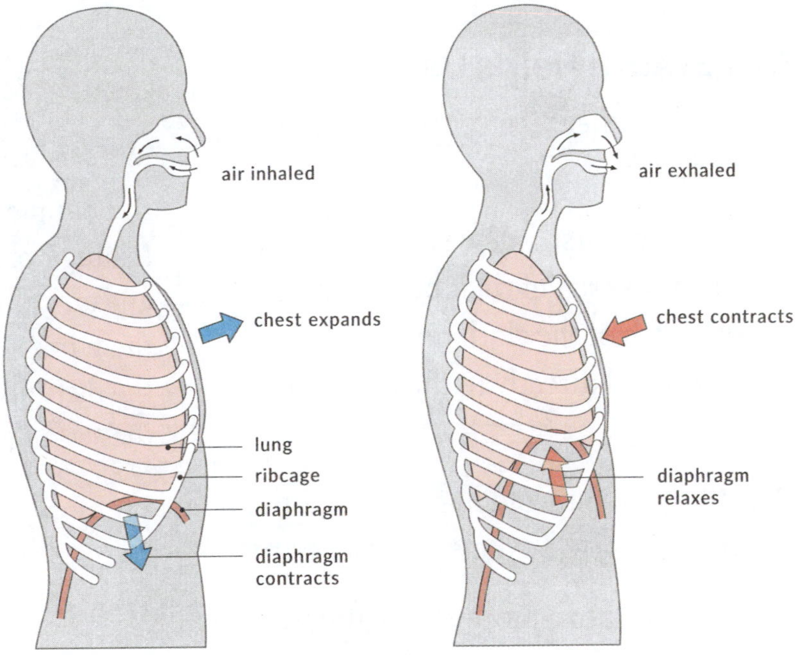

Breathing

Smart Skills

Observation — 21st Century Skills

Using a measuring tape, measure the chest of your partner after inhaling air and then after exhaling air. Switch the role and ask your partner to do the same. Note down the measurements and compare. In which case does the chest measure more?

Breath is Hot and Moist

The air we blow out from our mouth contains moisture. When warm air from our mouth touches cold objects like glass, it condenses and forms tiny droplets of water that gather and form a cloudy layer on an object. After some time, the cool water droplets evaporate at room temperature and disappear from the surface. Hot air rises because it is lighter than cold air.

Give It a Shot

E

Using a timer, note down the number of times you breathe in a minute when you are resting, walking, swimming, or skipping for three days.

	Resting	Walking	Swimming	Skipping
Day 1				
Day 2				
Day 3				

Our Breath Helps Us

The air we exhale can cool down hot milk, tea or soup.

While giving first aid, we can exhale air into a handkerchief till it becomes warm. The warmth of the cloth relieves pain when applied directly to the hurt part of the body.

Breathing on our cold hands makes them warm because the exhaled air is warmer.

Blowing air into a piece of burning wood while cooking increases the supply of oxygen and helps the wood to burn.

Musical instruments such as flutes and mouth organs are played by blowing air into them.

Smart Skills

Creative thinking

21ST CENTURY SKILLS

Materials needed: Old magazines and glue

Cut out pictures or advertisements related to lungs, oxygen, cold and cough remedies, and air pollution from old magazines. Paste them in a scrapbook. In groups, compare the pictures you found. Write which of these things assist or hinder breathing.

Picture Study

- What is the girl doing?
- How does it help us?

Breathing Well

The nose and the mouth are two passageways to our lungs. We breathe through our mouths when we have a cold. While exercising, or during a physical activity, breathing through the mouth supplies more oxygen to the muscles. Yet breathing through the mouth, especially while sleeping, can affect our health. We should try to always inhale through our nose as air is filtered here before entering our lungs.

Fitness combined with a healthy and balanced diet is the secret to a healthy life. We should practise deep breathing exercises. It helps us in the following ways:

- Releases tension
- Relaxes mind and body
- Improves posture
- Strengthens lungs
- Improves digestion

Skilling Up

Critical thinking

21ST CENTURY SKILLS

- Why is it not good to cover your head while sleeping?
- Why do people ask you to breathe in and breathe out when you are angry?
- When is it okay to breathe through your mouth?

What We Learnt

- All living things need water, food, air to live.
- Air supplies oxygen to our body
- Blowing air helps to make things cool and hot at the same time. It helps us play instruments.
- Fitness combined with a healthy and balanced diet is the secret to having a healthy life.
- Breathing is a process by which living things inhale oxygen and exhale carbon.
- Our breathing system consists of nose, trachea, bronchi, lungs, and diaphragm.
- Exchange of gases takes place inside lungs. Oxygen is absorbed and carbon dioxide is released.
- Breathing exercises help us stay healthy.

Think and Answer

A. Fill in the blanks.

1. Lungs .... (contract/ expand/ remains as it is) when we breathe in.
2. As oxygen is inhaled it converts food we eat into energy during .... (respiration/digestion/exhalation)
3. Lungs are protected by the .... (diaphragm/ribcage/chest).
4. The .... (alveoli/ribcage/diaphragm) is a strong muscle that lies below the lungs.
5. The .... (bronchi/nose/mouth) carry air into the lungs.

B. Write *T* for true and *F* for false.

1. Exhalation is the process of breathing out oxygen. ☐
2. Deep breathing releases tension and relaxes the mind and body. ☐
3. We should always breathe through our mouth. ☐
4. When the diaphragm relaxes, it moves up and the ribs move downward. ☐
5. The lungs are one of the largest organs in our body. ☐

C. Name them.

1. Trachea is also known as ....
2. Pair of spongy bag-like structures present in our chest ....
3. Before entering the lungs, the trachea branches out into ....
4. When water vapour changes into liquid on cooling ....
5. The sound of a heart beat can be heard by an instrument called ....

D. Answer these questions.

1. What is breathing?
2. Why do we breathe?
3. How are lungs protected?
4. What happens when the air carrying oxygen reaches lungs?
5. Give reasons:
    a. We should breathe through the nose and not through the mouth.
    b. Hot milk can be cooled down by blowing air.
    c. When we take bath in hot water, the mirrors in the bathroom turn hazy.

Cross Connect

HC CC

Pop bottle music

Fill some glass bottles with different amounts of water. Don't fill them till the brim. Blow gently across the top of the bottle so that you can hear a sound. Now, blow gently across all the bottles. They should all make different sounds. Why? This is because blowing air inside the bottle makes the water vibrate, creating the notes.

Web link

For more information, log on to:
https://cosmickids.com/five-fun-breathing-exercises-for-kids/

Last accessed on 30 August 2021

10. Helping Hands

Get Going

Dignity of Labour

10 REDUCED INEQUALITIES

Once when Gopal Krishna Gokhale visited Gandhiji in South Africa he found him ironing his handkerchief. Gokhale was not very sure of Gandhiji's ability to iron clothes well, but when he saw how perfectly Gandhiji had ironed his handkerchief he laughingly told Gandhiji that he was an 'expert *dhobhi!*'. When in a jail in South Africa, Gandhiji made a pair of sandals for General Smuts. Dignity of labour is to give respect to all kinds of work and to the people who do those work. No work is more important or superior than another or below one's self.

- Why are some kinds of work thought to be less important than others?
- What do we learn about Mahatma Gandhi from the this passage?

We need help from other people to complete many important tasks. This basic need for other peoples' help makes society friendly and **interdependent**. People who help us in our daily lives are known as **helpers**.

A maid comes to our house every day and helps us by cleaning the house. The gardener looks after the garden in our homes. Some of us have a driver to take us to office or other places. They are known as **domestic workers** as they help us in our homes.

Smart Skills

Creative thinking and Teamwork — 21ST CENTURY SKILLS

In groups make a duty roster to keep your classroom clean. Different students can have different duties with each one getting a duty at least once in the week. These could be cleaning the blackboard or white board, placing desks and chairs in the required manner, removing pencil shavings and waste food from the floor, recycling used paper or segregating waste in the classroom in separate bins. The group-wise duty chart can be pinned on the soft boards.

interdependent: dependent on each other

Community Services

We live in a community and for the proper functioning and organization of our community, we need **community helpers**.

In a community, there are people who do different types of work, such as clearing garbage, delivering letters and packages, guarding buildings, fixing traffic signals, putting out fires, guarding the country and taking care of city parks. A school bus driver and conductor take students to school every day where the teachers teach and guide the students. A washer-man or dhobhi washes and irons our school uniform as well as our father's or mother's office clothes. Postal workers, soldiers, painters, carpenters and *kabaadiwalas* are also our helpers. They live and work in the community. They are also known as **community workers**.

Firefighters

Postal worker

Skilling Up

Creative thinking

21ST CENTURY SKILLS

Saying Thank You

There are many helpers in our school such as cleaners, gardeners, guards, peons, bus drivers and conductors. Make a Thank You Card for any one of them using chart paper. Give it to that helper to let him or her know that you are grateful for their help.

Social Work

Work done by people to improve the conditions of the society and the people living in it is called **social work**. **Social workers** are trained persons who help bring in social change, development and work for the rights of those people and/or communities in our society who are not so educated or **privileged**. Social

Smart Skills

Life skills

21ST CENTURY SKILLS

Volunteering to help others can be done anywhere and at any age. Think of the ways you can volunteer both at home and school. Make a list of five volunteering activities in your notebook. Do you think you can learn important values while volunteering? If so, which values will you learn?

privileged: having special rights or advantages that most people do not have

workers can have different occupations and can work on their own or as part of an organisation. There are many government, non-government and other organisations involved in social work. In Class 3 you learnt about the Children's Foundation started by the Nobel Laureate Kailash Satyarthi, which is an NGO (Non-Government Organisation) working for the rights of children. Many times, people do social work without taking any money. They are called **volunteers.** They volunteer on their own or with an organisation to help the community and the people who need it most. Volunteers too are community helpers.

Matter of Fact

Mahatma Gandhi always spoke about the principle of **bread labour**. By this he meant that we should do physical work to fulfil our needs in return for the food, clothes and gifts that we receive. By doing our work ourselves we provide dignity to labour and remove the inequalities between manual and intellectual labour.

Kinds of Work

Different people are engaged in different types of occupations. Some jobs require us to use our mental ability and some require us to use our physical ability. Teachers and architects use their intellect to complete their jobs. This is called **intellectual labour**.

Jobs that require physical work are called **manual labour**. Farmers, electricians and sweepers do manual labour.

Smart Skills

Critical thinking

21ST CENTURY SKILLS

What would happen if all the sweepers and garbage pickers in the city decided to go on a strike? How can we reduce garbage in our homes?

Essential Services

Community helpers improve the quality of our lives and make it more comfortable by the services they provide. Some of these services affect our daily lives and are called **essential services**. Sweepers, newspaper vendors, milkman, vegetable vendors and grocers are some helpers that provide us essential services. Doctors, nurses, dentists, policemen and policewomen provide essential services necessary for us to live. During the COVID-19 pandemic

Vegetable vendor

bread labour: every person has to labour with his body for his food and clothing; **dignity:** worthy, honoured

lockdown when everyone was at home, the essential services workers continued to work despite the danger of being infected themselves. They were thus called **frontline warriors** for like soldiers they were fighting the coronavirus so that we could be safe in our homes. Imagine what life would be like if one or all of them stopped working?

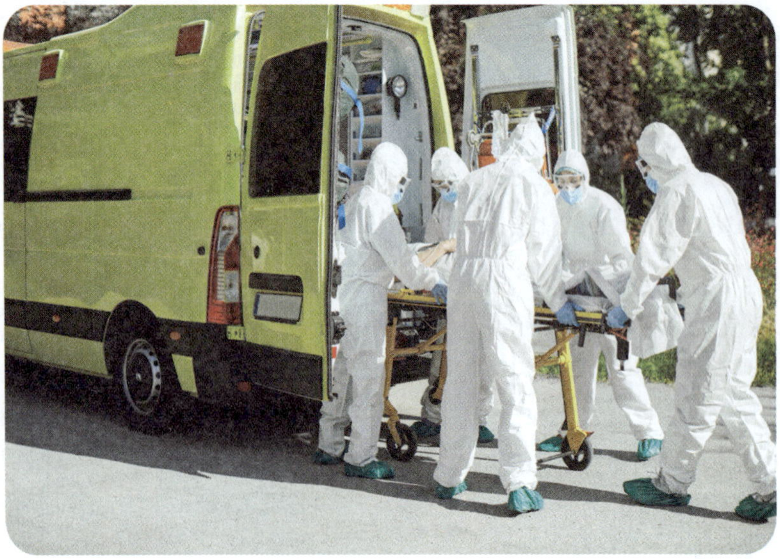

Frontline warriors

Dignity of Labour

Respect towards any kind of work and for the person who does it is known as **dignity of labour**. A feeling of **dignity** in the work one does give a person a sense of pride. It encourages her or him to enjoy what she or he is doing. All jobs should be respected equally, and no occupation should be considered **menial** or inferior or superior. We should not look down on people because of the work that they do. We should always remember to show **gratitude** and respect to those who help us and make our lives easier.

Give It a Shot

E

12 RESPONSIBLE CONSUMPTION AND PRODUCTION

What do you do with your textbooks when you are promoted to the next class? Do you sell them to the *kabaadiwala*? As a class, donate your old textbooks to your juniors.

Instead of throwing your old notebooks, separate the unused pages from your notebooks and spiral bind them to use them for rough work in the new class. Sell the remaining copies to the *kabaadiwala* to recycle paper.

menial: work that is often boring and low-paid; **gratitude:** the quality of being thankful

What We Learnt

- Respect for any kind of work and the person who does it is called dignity of labour.
- Jobs that require the use of mental ability are called intellectual labour. Jobs that require the use of physical ability are called manual labour.
- People who help us in our homes are called domestic helpers.
- People who help us in our daily lives are called helpers.
- Some of these community services affect our daily lives and are called essential services.
- People who help in the proper functioniong of the community are called community helpers.
- Work done by people to improve the conditions of the people is called social work.

Think and Answer

A. Fill in the blanks with the correct answers.

1. We call the .... if we have been robbed.
   a. friends b. police c. teacher d. doctor
2. A teacher ....
   a. catches thieves b. gives injection c. fixes broken toys d. helps children learn
3. We are taught that those who help us must also be given ....
   a. gifts b. clothes c. pity d. respect
4. Gandhiji spoke about the importance of doing physical work. He called this.........
   a. Manual labour b. bread labour c. intellectual labour d. social work
5. Some people consider certain jobs like cleaning toilets to be ....
   a. attractive b. important c. menial d. high paying

B. Put these helpers under the correct category of services they provide in the table given below.

1. Farmer 2. Doctor 3. Vegetable vendor 4. Housemaid 5. Sweeper
6. driver 7. Architect 8. Plumber 9. Gardener 10. Potter
11. Chef

Domestic Services	Community Services	Essential Services

C. Fill in the blanks.

1. No job is too .... or ....
2. Those who help make our lives easier need our .... and ....
3. Jobs that require the use of physical ability are called ....
4. Jobs that require the use of mental ability are called ....
5. Services that we need every day for the smooth running of our lives are called .... services.

D. Answer these questions.

1. Why do we need different people to do different jobs?
2. What do we learn from respecting every work?
3. What do you understand by dignity of labour?
4. What is the difference between social work and occupation?
5. What are essential services? Name some people who provide such services.

Cross Connect

With inputs from your EVS teacher, organise a Career Day for your class once every month. On this day, invite a helper or a provider of a service to come to your class and speak about their profession and the work they do. You can invite the helpers from your school or from the city in which you live. In groups be responsible for the entire organisation of the Career Day. This will mean identifying the speaker, making invitation cards, decorating your classroom, deciding on the day and time of the talk, introducing the speaker and thanking him or her. All of this should be done completely by you. This can be done online as well.

Web link

For more information, log on to:

https://www.hindustantimes.com/india-news/lucknow-engineer-turns-kabadiwala-in-online-avatar-with-app-to-sell-scrap-101616568722524.html

Last accessed on 30 August 2021

11. Be Healthy

Get Going

Healthy Immune System

3 GOOD HEALTH AND WELL-BEING

In recent times you may have heard that doctors and scientists telling everyone to have a healthy immune system. The body system that helps fight off diseases is called immune system. It helps in protecting the body from any disease. The food we eat is very important, it should be balanced and nutritious. It will keep us healthy and will increase our immunity. Along with eating healthy, balanced meal and snacks we need to do regular physical activity and need to wash our hands often.

- Which disease has disturbed the lives of people all over the world?
- What precautions are you taking?
- What kind of food are you taking?

Food is an essential and important part of everyone's life. It makes our body work, grow and repair itself. Food gives us the energy and nutrients to do day-to-day activities such as going to school, playing, studying, dancing, walking and swimming. We should eat healthy food in order to stay fit. We should eat lots of nutritious food, including fruits, vegetables, protein rich foods, yogurt, seeds and nuts.

Matter of Fact

Did you know tomato is the most popular and most consumed fruit in the world? It's a key ingredient used in countless cuisines. It is the most versatile fruit, which is used in sauces, soups, salads, for garnishing and even as juices.

Food Habits

India is a country of **diverse** food habits. Different types of food items are found in different regions. The type of food consumed is mainly based on the location, climate, crops grown, cultural

diverse: a great deal of variety

habits and traditions. Indian food is unique because of the different types of ingredients used to cook different dishes, namely, grains, pulses, spices, oilseeds, fruits and vegetables.

In places located near a river or a sea, like Kerala, West Bengal and Assam, fish is a popular food item. Wheat grows in places with a cool and moist climate. It is the **staple** food of the people of northern and central states such as Punjab, Uttar Pradesh, Haryana, Gujarat and Madhya Pradesh. Rice is grown in West Bengal, Assam and Kerala. It is the staple food of these states. Fish and meat form an important part of the cuisine of eastern and northeastern India. Along with this, a variety of vegetables, mostly found only in those regions, are eaten. In the southern part of India, the use of fresh coconut, curry leaves and mustard seeds in their cooking is common.

Smart Skills — Information literacy — 21ST CENTURY SKILLS

- Ask your grandparents what they ate when they were young.
- What were the names of the dishes cooked?
- Make a list of these food items and compare them to the food items you eat.

Fish curry and rice

Dhokla

Biryani

There has been a shift from our traditional food habits to food that lack nutrients we need. **Junk food** like pizzas, burgers, aerated drinks and other street food, typically deep fried, have a lot of calories and very little nutritional value.

Nutrients in Food

A **nutrient** is a substance found in food, which provides **nourishment** and helps the body to grow. Nutrients give us energy, help us to grow and protect us from diseases. Five types of nutrients, namely proteins, carbohydrates, fats, vitamins and minerals are present in food in varying quantities.

Smart Skills — Critical thinking — 21ST CENTURY SKILLS

- Why do sportspersons consume energy drinks frequently during matches?
- Do you always finish your meal served?

staple: an important food of a region; **nourishment:** food necessary for growth and health

- **Proteins** are necessary for growth and repair of the body. They also help in building muscles. Food items rich in proteins are eggs, beans, pulses, groundnuts, nuts, milk, fish, meat and chicken.
- **Carbohydrates** provide energy to our body. Sugar and starchy food like rice, chapati, potato and banana are rich sources of carbohydrates.
- **Fats** provide energy to the body. Oils, butter, ghee and nuts are rich sources of fats.
- **Vitamins** protect our body against diseases. Fruits and vegetables have ample quantities of vitamins.
- **Minerals** help in the physical and mental development of the body. They keep our teeth and bones strong and healthy. Milk, cheese, eggs, fresh fruits and vegetables are some food items rich in minerals. Iron, calcium and iodine are some examples of minerals.

Proteins

Carbohydrates

Nuts

Balanced Diet

The food that we eat on a regular basis is called our **diet**. A diet that provides all the nutrients in the right quantity is called a **balanced diet**. A balanced diet is complete only when we drink sufficient water in a day and eat the right amount of roughage. **Roughage** is the indigestible portion of plant food.

Give It a Shot

E

In groups, interview a few students of your age group. Find out their daily routine, favourite food and activities. Discuss whether they take a balanced diet and the changes they should make to their diet. Share your findings through a PowerPoint presentation.

Deficiency diseases

Taking nutrients in less quantity or not taking any one nutrient for a long time causes diseases. A disease caused by the lack of a nutrient in our diet is called a **deficiency disease**.

The following table shows some common deficiency diseases, their symptoms and the food that should be taken to prevent them.

Deficiency Diseases	Symptoms	Nutrients	Food Sources
Night blindness	Inability to see in dim light	Vitamin A	Green vegetables, carrots, papayas, yellow pumpkins and milk
Beriberi	Nerve disorders that affect muscles and the heart	Vitamin B	Green leafy vegetables, whole grains, fruits and milk
Scurvy	Swollen and bleeding gums	Vitamin C	Lemons, oranges and tomatoes
Rickets	Weak bones	Vitamin D	Sunlight, milk, fish and egg yolk
Anaemia	Weakness, loss of weight and appetite	Iron	Meat, green leafy vegetables and milk
Goitre	Swelling in the neck glands	Iodine	Iodised salt, milk and eggs
Kwashiorkor	Tiredness, swollen belly	Protein	Pulses, meat and egg

Scarcity of Food

Food that we eat every day determines how well our body functions. We need to eat the right amount of food to keep ourselves fit and healthy. However, there are millions of people who are malnourished due to scarcity of food.

Food scarcity can be caused in the event of a **calamity** or natural disaster like flood, drought, tsunami or an earthquake. It can also occur due to human **negligence**, for instance, improper storage of food and food wastage.

Picture Study

- Have you ever thought what happens to the leftover food after a party?
- What do you do with the left over food in your home?

Famines and malnutrition

An acute shortage of food is called a **famine**. It is caused by several factors like war, rise in food prices, crop failure, population imbalance, or government policies. **Malnutrition**, hunger, widespread diseases and deaths are some effects of famine. Malnutrition is a lack of proper nutrition and is caused by not having enough to eat. Not eating enough nutrients or being unable to absorb the nutrients one consumes, can also cause malnutrition.

calamity: an adverse event like earthquake, flood, drought, tsunami; **negligence:** inability to take proper care

We can prevent wastage of food by following some simple rules.

- Cook food in measured amounts.
- Leftover food can be stored properly and eaten the next day.
- Take small quantities of food on your plate so that you can finish it.
- Preserve food to keep it from getting spoilt.
- Buy food in small amounts.

Smart Skills

Communication

21ST CENTURY SKILLS

A survey declares that India wastes as much food as the United Kingdom consumes. According to the United Nations Development Programme, almost 40 percent of the food produced in India goes waste. Some restaurants in India employ food controllers to check food spoilage or wastage.

2 ZERO HUNGER

- What do you think hotels and restaurants should do with the extra food so that it is not wasted? Discuss in class.

Bengal famine of 1943: In 1943, there was a major famine in the Bengal Presidency, which caused the deaths of approximately 2.1 million people. It occurred during the Second World War when India was under the control of the British. A year prior to the famine, Japan conquered Burma, which was a rice exporter to India. Rice stopped coming from Burma, leading to severe food shortage in Bengal.

The British, who fought against Japan, feared that Japan would enter India through Bengal. They burned the rice fields to prevent the Japanese from using them. This worsened the food shortage and caused panic. People **hoarded** rice in large quantities. The price of rice in Dacca (now Dhaka) increased four times its original price in the period from March to October 1943. People suffered immensely due to **starvation**, malaria and other diseases, followed by malnutrition, displacement of population, unsanitary conditions and lack of health care.

Skilling Up

Life skills

21ST CENTURY SKILLS

While buying food items sold in bottles, tins, or packets, check and make a list of the following:

- Name of the item
- Ingredients used
- Date of manufacture
- Expiry date
- Max retail price (MRP)
- Any mark of quality, like AGMARK

Why is it important to know these details about packaged food items?

hoard: a collection of money, food, valuable objects; **starvation:** the state in which somebody suffers or dies because they have no food

What We Learnt

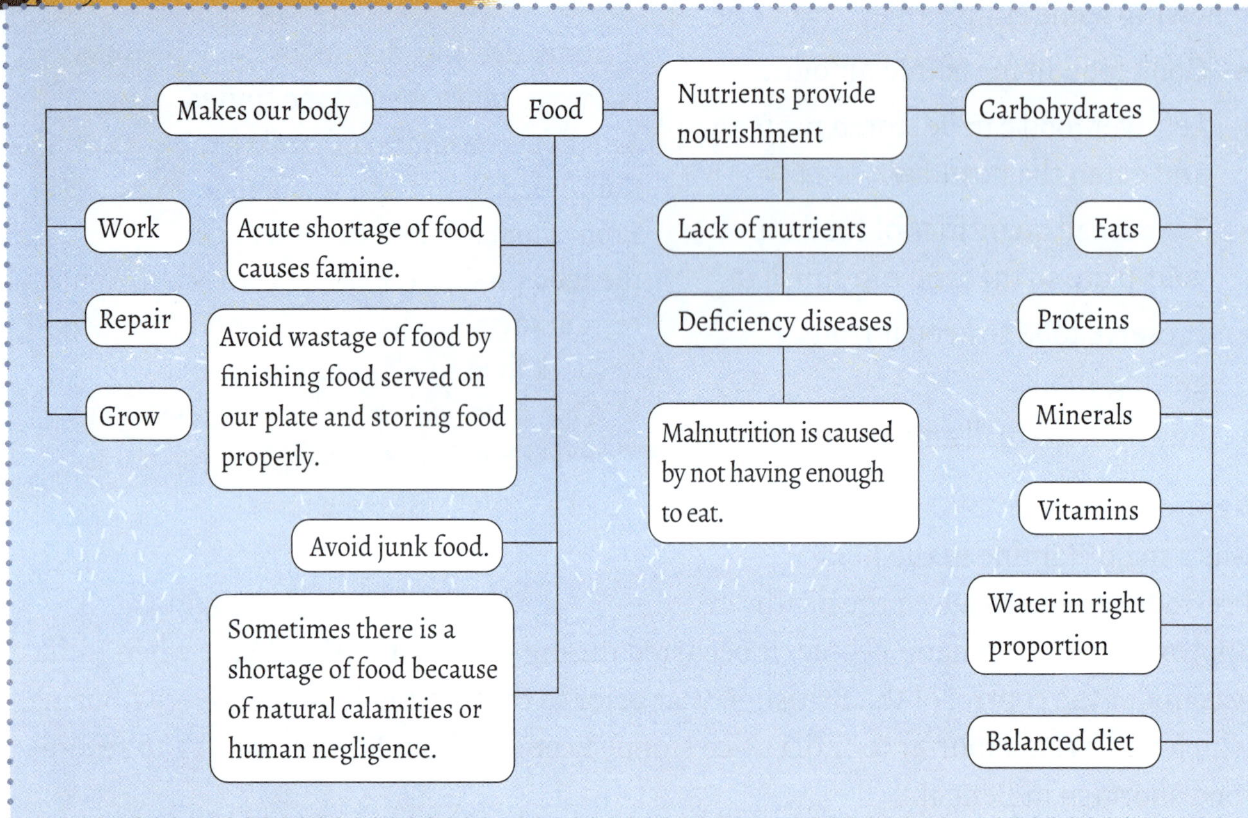

Think and Answer

A. Fill in the blanks with the correct answers.

1. Fresh coconut, curry leaves and mustard seeds are used in their cooking in .... (eastern/northern/southern) parts of India.
2. Carbohydrates like sugar and starchy food provide .... (growth/protection/energy) to our body.
3. Rice is grown in .... (Punjab/Kerala/Uttar Pradesh).
4. Beriberi is caused due to deficiency of .... (iron/protein/vitamin B).
5. An acute .... (wastage/shortage/usage) of food is called famine.

B. Fill in the blanks.

1. The deficiency of iron causes ....
2. Night blindness is caused by the deficiency of...................................... .
3. Goitre is caused by the deficiency of ....
4. .... is a disease caused by deficiency of protein.
5. Scurvy is a disease caused by deficiency of ....

C. Write T for true and F for false.

1. Deficiency of vitamins causes beriberi.
2. Oil, butter and fruits are carbohydrates.
3. Junk food provides ample quantities of vitamins and minerals to the body.
4. When any one or more nutrients are not consumed for a long time, it results in deficiency diseases.
5. Deficiency of vitamins causes anaemia.

D. Answer these questions.

1. Why are vitamins important for us?
2. What are food habits? Give examples of food habits of two regions in India.
3. What are nutrients?
4. What causes scarcity of food?
5. Name the causes and symptoms of these diseases:
   a. Kwashiorkor b. Anaemia c. Goitre
6. Define balanced diet and nutrition.

Cross Connect

Painting with Coffee

Materials Required: Paper, pencil, paint brushes, instant coffee and water.

Draw before you start painting. Dissolve some instant coffee in hot water. Darker hues will require less water than the lighter shades. Coffee lightens when it dries, so you will need to go over your paper quite a bit until you reach the desired appearance. Add the next layer once the previous layer is completely dry.

Web link

For more information, log on to:
https://www.superkidsnutrition.com/healthy-meal-plan-for-kids-7-to-8-years-old/

Last accessed on 30 August 2021

12. Respect Food

Unit 4: My Needs

Get Going

Tick the food which should be kept in the refrigerator.

Sandwich ☐

Paneer masala ☐

Biscuits ☐

Juice ☐

Chips ☐

Fruits ☐

Dry fruits ☐

How do you know food is spoilt?

Spoilage of Food

Food spoilage is a disagreeable change in a food item's normal state. When food is exposed to air or **moisture** for a long time, it gets spoilt. It develops a foul odour, changes in colour, becomes slimy or develops a furry layer. These changes can be detected by smell, taste, touch or sight. Food gets spoilt if it is not stored or packed properly. If some food items like fish, meat, milk, bread, tomatoes and potatoes are not eaten soon, they get spoilt. Other food items can be stored for a longer period of time, but all food items eventually **decompose**.

Picture Study

When does milk smell bad? Why does this happen?

moisture: small amounts of water found in the air and food; **decompose:** to be destroyed gradually by natural processes

There are two types of food. These are **perishable** and **non-perishable** food. Food that gets spoilt quickly is known as perishable food. Fruits, vegetables, milk and milk products are some examples of perishable food. Food that lasts for a longer period is known as non-perishable food. Wheat, cereals and nuts are examples of non-perishable food.

How Food Spoils

Very tiny living things called **microbes** live amongst us. They are so small that they cannot be seen by the naked eye. These microbes, especially bacteria and fungi, can spoil the food. They grow well in places where the moisture content is high. So air, moisture, microbes, insects, rodents, physical damage and temperature are responsible for spoilage of food.

Smart Skills

Information literacy

21ST CENTURY SKILLS

Meghna and her family were travelling by train from Mumbai to Chennai during the rainy season. Her mom had packed different food items. Find out:

- What type of food would she pack and why?
- Why did Meghna pack grapes instead of raisins?

Give It a Shot

E

Experiment

Things needed: Two slices of bread, half a cup of water, a plate or a tiffin box and a jar.

Method: Sprinkle a little water on one slice of bread and place it on a plate or in a tiffin box. Put the other slice of bread in a jar and tightly close the lid. Observe both for a week.

Observations

- What happens to the slice of bread on the plate?
- What happens to the slice of bread kept in the jar?
- Why do you think it happened?

Food Preservation

Food preservation is the process of storing food to keep it from getting spoilt. The taste of the food and its nutritional value is maintained through preservation. **Preservation** of food prevents diseases or food poisoning. Symptoms of food poisoning are vomiting, nausea, fever, diarrhoea and stomach

Dehydrated kiwis

preservation: the process of preventing food from getting spoilt

ache. Food is preserved for other reasons too. Sometimes, food needs to be transported to other areas where it is not grown. To maintain its taste and nutritional value, it should be preserved. If we want to make off-season fruits and vegetables available to people throughout the year, we must preserve them. There are many methods of food preservation.

Skilling Up

Problem-solving

21ST CENTURY SKILLS

- Is it okay to leave food in your tiffin box? Why?
- Why does food get spoilt faster in summer?
- Have you ever fallen sick after eating spoilt food? Discuss how you felt.

Freezing and refrigeration: Freezing helps to preserve food from the time it is prepared till the time it is consumed. Freezing and refrigerating food involves storing food at a temperature lower than that needed for bacteria to grow. This keeps the food fresh.

Drying: Drying removes moisture from food and prevents the growth of microbes. Dates and raisins are preserved as dry fruits.

Freeze-drying: Another method where food is frozen at a very low temperature, then dried by removing moisture from food is freeze-drying. A sealed, freeze-dried food prevents the **reabsorption** of moisture and can be stored without refrigeration for a long time. Coffee, fruits, juices, vegetables, meat, fish and seafood can be freeze dried.

Pasteurisation: This technique, invented by a French scientist **Louis Pasteur**, is used to preserve milk and other food items. Milk is heated to a high temperature and then quickly cooled before bottling or packaging. This kills the microbes and does not affect the flavour of the milk.

Boiling milk

Canning: Canning is a safe and an important method of preserving food. In this method, food items are placed in air-tight jars or containers and heated to a temperature that kills microbes. During the heating process, air is driven out of the container and as it cools, a vacuum is formed inside the container and it is sealed. Fruits, vegetables, jams and pickles are preserved by canning.

reabsorption: absorbing again

Smart Skills

Life skills

21ST CENTURY SKILLS

Speak with your grandparents or elders in the family and find out how they preserved food when there were no refrigerators. Write down the different methods and create a chart on it.

Pickling: In this method, vinegar, salt and oil are added to raw or cooked vegetables and fruits, which slows down the growth of microbes.

Pickling

Salting or curing: Salting draws out moisture from the food and kills the bacteria present in it. In cold temperatures, meat is salted so that it does not spoil. Cured meat can last for months.

Sugaring: Sugaring is the process in which food is first dried and then sugar is added. This sugar can be crystalline in the form of raw sugar, or in the form of sugary liquids like honey, syrup or **molasses**. The process of sugaring is used in jellies, jams and murabbas to preserve fruits and vegetables, for example strawberry, mixed fruit, apple jams, Indian gooseberry, ash pumpkin and carrot murabbas.

Jams

Pickling, salting and sugaring not only help to preserve food, but also add flavour to the food. One must respect food and use few of these methods to prevent food from spoiling.

Smart Skills

Analysis and Communication

21ST CENTURY SKILLS

Divide the class in two groups. Make a list of a few food items such as fruits, vegetables, cereals and one cooked food in class. Suggest one method of preserving them. Find out another modern way of food preservation used around the world. Have a class discussion on the topic 'Wastage of food can be controlled by preservation'.

molasses: a thick black syrup made from sugar

What We Learnt

- **Food**
  - **Food spoilage**
    - When food is exposed to air or moisture for a long time, it gets spoilt.
    - Spoilt food develops a foul order, changes in colour, becomes slimy or develops a furry layer.
    - Food that gets spoilt quickly is known as perishable food.
    - Food that does not spoil quickly is known as non-perishable food.
  - **Food preservation**
    - We can prevent spoilage of food by preserving it.
  - The methods of food preservation are
    - Refrigeration
    - Drying
    - Freeze drying
    - Canning
    - Pasteurisation
    - Pickling
    - Salting and sugaring

Think and Answer

A. Fill in the blanks with the correct answers.

1. Milk can be kept fresh by ....
   (canning/drying/pasteurisation)
2. Fruits and vegetables are preserved at home by ....
   (cutting/refrigeration/canning/pasteurisation)
3. The taste of the food and its nutritional value is maintained through ....
   (preservation/spoilage/absorption)
4. .... is used to preserve jams or murabbas, fruits and vegetables.
   (Salting/Sugaring/Pickling)
5. .... removes moisture from food and prevents the growth of microbes.
   (Freezing/Salting/Sugaring)

B. Write *T* for true and *F* for false.

1. Food usually gets spoilt in winter. ☐
2. Food kept in air-tight containers spoils faster. ☐
3. Salt and oil are preservatives. ☐
4. Foods that do not get spoilt easily are known as perishable foods. ☐
5. Vinegar is a preservative and it also adds flavour to food. ☐

C. Unscramble the following words.

1. NANGINC ....
2. RAINVEG ....
3. GIPLINCK ....
4. INGLAST ....

D. Answer these questions.

1. What happens when we eat spoilt food?
2. Give two examples of perishable and non-perishable foods.
3. What is food spoilage? How is it caused?
4. What is food preservation?
5. Explain four methods of food preservation.

Cross Connect

Make Pickled Onions

Take 10 to 15 baby onions. With the help of an adult, slice or peel the onions and place them in the strainer. Pour 2 to 3 cups of boiling water on the sliced onions. Add 1 tablespoon of sugar and salt in a glass jar and pour 3 to 4 cups of white vinegar in the jar. Add one red chilli, a sprig of thyme, two garlic pods and peppercorns. Add the sliced onions in the jar. Keep it aside for 30 minutes. The pickled onions are ready!

Web link

For more information, log on to:
https://www.nationalgeographic.com/environment/article/partner-content-packaging-for-good

Last accessed on 30 August 2021

13. World Inside

Get Going

Which is your favourite dish? Why?

Chole Bhature

Kheer

Idli Sambar

Have you ever wondered what happens to the food after you eat it? When we eat our favourite dish, it is not in a form that the body can use as a source of energy. All that we eat, or drink, needs to be converted into small nutrients, and then they are absorbed into the bloodstream and are transported throughout the body.

Our body gets nutrients from the food that we eat. Food we eat is broken down into simple substances so that the body can get the nutrients present in it. The process of the breakdown of complex food into simple food **molecules** that can be easily absorbed by the body is called **digestion**.

Digestive System

Food enters our body and passes through many organs to get digested. These organs that work together to digest our food, makes up the **digestive system**. Food begins its journey from the mouth, then passes through the food pipe, the stomach, the small intestine and finally to the large intestine. Digestion involves the crushing and mashing of

Matter of Fact

Enzymes help in the chemical reactions in the body. The digestive enzymes break down fat, proteins, and carbohydrates so that food can be easily absorbed. There are three main types of digestive enzymes: proteases, lipases and amylases.

molecules: a very small particles

food as well as breaking down of food by certain enzymes produced by our body. Each stage of digestion is important and prepares food for the next stage. **Anxiety** and emotions like anger and sadness can affect the digestion of food.

Smart Skills

Research

21ST CENTURY SKILLS

- Who are gastroenterologists? How are they helpful to us?
- Food can be eaten and digested even if a person stands on his head. Find out how.

Process of digestion

The process of digestion starts even before the food enters the mouth. Often, when we think of our favourite food or when we see it, we begin to salivate. This is because the brain sends signals to the body to be prepared for food.

Picture Study

- What happens to the food in the mouth?
- Why should we eat only healthy food?

Mouth: The digestive system begins with the mouth where the **teeth** and **tongue** work together. The teeth help to chew, thus breaking the food into smaller pieces.

The **tongue** is the muscular organ in the mouth which is used for tasting and swallowing. Thousands of taste buds cover its surface. These taste buds help us identify different tastes like sweet, sour, salty and bitter.

The **salivary glands** present near the tongue secrete **saliva** which is a watery liquid secreted into the mouth. It keeps the mouth wet, moistens the food and mixes it to form a paste. The saliva contains an enzyme that breaks down the carbohydrate in the food like rice to sugar.

Oesophagus: Food from the mouth enters a hollow tube called the **oesophagus** or **food pipe**. The muscles of the oesophagus contract and relax to push the food to the stomach.

Stomach: The stomach muscles grind and **churn** the food into a semi-fluid state. The digestive juices secreted by the stomach walls contain enzymes, which further break down the food into proteins, carbohydrates, and fats in our stomach. The food then passes to the small intestine.

anxiety: a feeling of nervousness or worry; **churn:** to move about vigorously

Small intestine: The small intestine is a long muscular tube that mixes food with enzymes. The useful nutrients from the digested food are absorbed by the walls of the small intestine. These nutrients are then absorbed by the blood vessels, which carry them to different parts of the body. Digestion of the food is completed here.

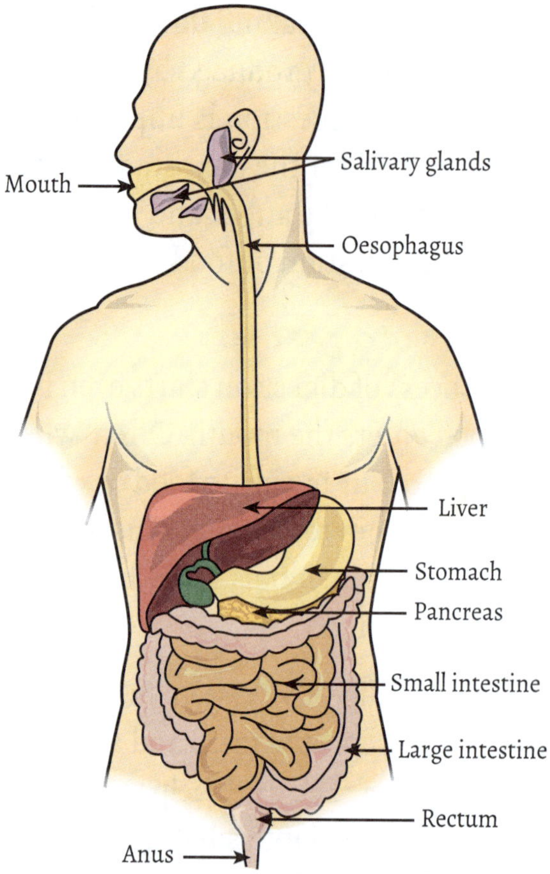

Human digestive system

Large intestine: The undigested food enters the large intestine where the water and minerals are absorbed. The undigested food then gets converted into solid waste, which passes into the **rectum** as faeces. The faeces exit the body through an opening called **anus**.

Why We Need Glucose

Glucose is a simple sugar. It is absorbed by blood and it gives instant energy to the body. Glucose can be taken orally. When a sick person is unable to eat and digest the food, the person becomes weak and dizzy. It is important to directly inject fluid containing glucose to the blood of the sick person (patient). This is also known as **glucose drip**, which helps the body regain instant energy and function normally.

Smart Skills

Critical thinking

21ST CENTURY SKILLS

- Why should we not sleep immediately after eating?
- Why should we not talk while eating?
- Why is food cooked at home is better than junk food?

Give It a Shot

E

Things required: Slices of bread or roti

Method:

- Take a bite of the roti or bread and chew it two to three times and swallow it.
- Take another bite and chew it slowly many times.

In which method will food taste better, and be easier to digest and why?

Importance of Water

Water is essential for good health.

- Water and other liquids helps the body absorb nutrients.
- Drinking water prevents **constipation**.
- Drinking water keeps the body hydrated and makes up for the loss of water through sweating, breathing and digestion.
- Children should drink enough water as they constantly sweat during warm weather or while doing physical activities.
- Children between 4 to 13 years of age should drink about 4 to 8 glasses of water in a day.

Smart Skills — Life skills — 21ST CENTURY SKILLS

3 GOOD HEALTH AND WELL-BEING

Find out the food, quantity and number of meals eaten by people of different age groups mentioned below. You can ask an adult to help.

- Toddlers (age group 1–2 years)
- Children of your age (10 years)
- Parents (30–40 years)
- Grandparents (60–70 years)

Find out the activities that they do throughout the day and make a chart. Identify the differences in the food eaten and their daily activities.

Healthy and Good Eating Habits

We should eat everything in the right amount. Some good eating habits we should follow are:

- Eat lots of green vegetables and fruits.
- Eat meals at the right time.
- Never skip breakfast.
- Eat food rich in fibres (roughage) as it helps to control the movement of food in the digestive system. It also helps in elimination of waste.
- Take small bites of food while eating and chew it properly.
- Drink at least 6 to 8 glasses of water every day.
- Avoid going to bed immediately after eating as it takes four hours for the food to get digested in the stomach.

Eating healthy

There are many children in our country who do not get enough food to eat. So we should not waste food by not eating and throwing away leftovers.

constipation: the condition of being unable to get rid of waste material from the body easily

Skilling Up

Problem-solving

21ST CENTURY SKILLS

- How can schools help those who do not have enough to eat? Discuss this in groups in the class.
- Make a poster to spread awareness about this issue.

What We Learnt

Digestion

The process of breakdown of complex food into simple food molecules that can be easily absorbed by the body is called digestion.

Teeth help in chewing, tongue helps in tasting and saliva breaks down carbohydrates present in the food to sugar.

Partial digestion of food occurs in the stomach and is completed in the small intestine.

After digestion is completed in the small intestine, absorption takes place. The blood absorbs the nutrients present in the food and sends these to all parts of the body.

We should follow healthy and good eating habits.

Think and Answer

A. Name them.

1. This muscle grinds and churns the food into semi-fluid state. ....
2. This muscular organ is used for tasting and swallowing. ....
3. The undigested food enters here, where water and minerals are absorbed ....
4. Digestion of the food is completed here. ....
5. These help to chew and break down food into smaller pieces. ....

B. Fill in the blanks with the correct answers.

1. Saliva is produced by the .... (pancreas/stomach/salivary glands)
2. The digested food is absorbed in the blood stream through the walls of the .... (oesophagus/stomach/small intestine).

3. Children between 4 to 13 years of age should drink .... (4 to 8/ 2 to 5/ 8 to 10) glasses of water in a day.
4. Drinking water prevents .... (digestion/constipation/rehydration).
5. .... (milk/roughage/both) helps in elimination of waste.

C. Write *T* for true and *F* for false.

1. The small intestine is a small muscular tube. ☐
2. The stomach muscles ground and churn the food into a semi-fluid state. ☐
3. Chewing is not a part of digestion. ☐
4. The small intestine is a very small part of the digestive system. ☐
5. Glucose helps the body to reclaim instant energy. ☐

D. Answer these questions.

1. What happens to the food in the stomach?
2. What is the importance of the large intestine?
3. What is digestion. Define the process of digestion.
4. What are some of the healthy and good eating habits.
5. What is the function of water in digestion?
6. How does saliva help in digestion?

Cross Connect

Some food is difficult to digest while some food is easy to digest. Talk to the adults in your house and list three food items in each category. Ask your friends from other regions of the country to do the same. Compare the lists and see which food items are considered easy to digest across the country.

Web link

For more information, log on to:
https://www.natgeokids.com/uk/discover/science/general-science/your-digestive-system/

Last accessed on 30 August 2021

Unit 4: My Needs

14. Magic Drink

Get Going

Water is Important

All living things need water to survive, either as a habitat, for drinking or cleaning. Water makes up more than half of our body weight. In India water is considered a holy drink. We have learnt that in ancient days, people worshipped water. Even today many rivers of our country are worshipped.

Ganga

- Name any three important rivers of India?
- Which is the national river of India?
- Name traditional containers of storing drinking water which are still used in many homes.

Water is an important natural, **renewable** resource. Like air and soil, water is essential for life on Earth. Plants, human beings, animals and even microbes need water to live.

Sources of Water

Most of the water present on Earth is found in the oceans and seas. However, this is **saline** water and is unsuitable for drinking. Only three per cent of the water on Earth is fit for drinking. It is called **freshwater** and is found in rivers, lakes, ponds and glaciers. It is also called **surface water**.

Water well

Freshwater is also found deep inside the Earth in the spaces between the soil and the rocks as **groundwater**. The top level of groundwater is called **water table**. The water in wells and springs comes from groundwater.

Rain is the main source of water on the Earth. Rainwater fills the rivers, lakes and ponds.

renewable: capable of being replaced; **saline:** containing salt

Some of this rainwater gets absorbed by the Earth and gets stored as groundwater. Trees and plants absorb groundwater through their roots. People use wells, hand pumps and tube wells to draw groundwater.

Hot water spring

Sometimes, the groundwater naturally pushes itself to the surface of the Earth forming a **spring**. Hot springs are formed when groundwater gets heated. Then water flows over hot volcanic rocks inside the surface of the Earth before emerging from the ground. This is why water is hot.

Smart Skills

Digital literacy

21ST CENTURY SKILLS

In groups, prepare a PowerPoint presentation on hot springs of India. Name four popular hot springs of India and places where they are found. Find out about each of them.

In cities, water reaches our homes through pipelines. Water from a river or underground water is purified and stored in large tanks.

Electric pumps are used at pump stations to transfer the water from these tanks to our homes through pipelines. Thus, people in cities do not have to walk far to get water.

Today, in many villages too, people get water in their homes through pipelines. However, there are still many villages and urban slums of India where women have to walk very far to fetch water from the village well or the local hand pump. They stand for many hours in long queues and wait for their turn to fill buckets and pots with water for their daily use.

Picture Study

Why are the women carrying pots on their heads? What is in the pots?

Properties of Water

We know that water is a colourless, tasteless and odourless liquid. It does not have a fixed shape. Water can flow easily and takes the shape of any container. It exists in three states: solid-ice, liquid-water, and gas-water vapour or steam.

Let us now learn a few more properties of water.

Universal solvent

Water can dissolve a variety of different substances, which is why it is such a good solvent. It is called the **universal solvent** because it dissolves more substances than any other liquid. The ability to dissolve a substance is called its **solubility**. The substance which is being dissolved is called **solute**. Salt and sugar are some examples. The liquid in which a solute is dissolved to form a solution is known as **solvent.** Water, milk and juice are some examples. The substances that dissolve in water are known as **soluble substances**. Sugar, salt and soap are some examples. The substances that do not dissolve are called **insoluble substances**. Chalk powder, sand, leaves and oil are some examples.

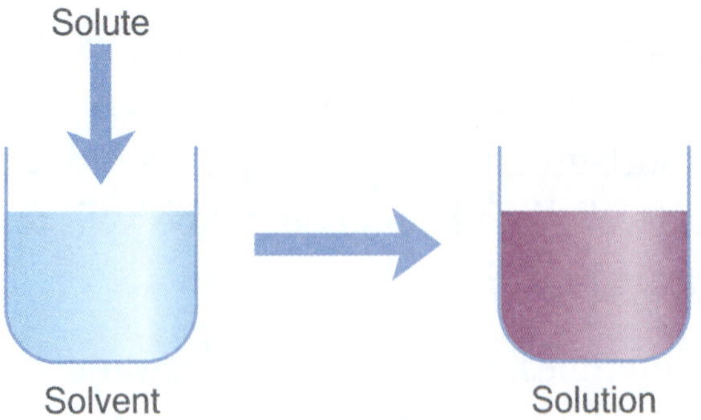

Solubility

Sink or float

There are objects which sink or float as soon as they are dropped in water. The **density** of an object determines whether it will float or sink in another substance. An object will float if it is less dense than water, when placed in it. The fact that ice floats in water is a bit strange, because most substances are denser when they are solids. Water, however, reaches its maximum density at 4.4 °C. As water cools and freezes further till 0°C, it becomes less dense. Ice floats because it is less dense than water.

Ice floats on water

Water never mixes with oil

Some things just don't get along well with each other. The molecules of water are packed densely. This means if we take equal parts of water and oil, there will be more molecules of water than oil. So, water will always sink underneath the oil. You can mix oil and water and shake as hard as you like but they'll never mix with each other.

Oil floats on water

When soap is added to oil and water, they don't separate like they did when they were the only two items in the glass. The soap is attracted to both the oil and the water and helps them both mix and stay mixed together. This same effect happens when you are washing dishes. The oil and grease on the dirty dishes is attached to the dish soap and water is used to wash them. Detergents and soaps help us to remove oil and dirt from utensils and our bodies.

density: how thick a solid, liquid or gas is

Give It a Shot

E

Observe and note down.

1. Take four glasses, a jug of water and spoons. Pour water in all the four glasses. Add chalk powder, salt, sugar and oil in four different glasses and stir.

Water + Sugar | Water + Salt | Water + Oil | Water + Chalk powder

2. Take a bowl of water and drop a nail, a leaf, a ping pong ball, a chalk, a paper clip and a marble.

Glass jar with a lid | 1 cup of water | food colour | 2 teaspoons of liquid dish soap

3. Keep a glass jar with a lid, one cup of water, food colour, one cup of oil and two teaspoons of liquid dish soap. Start by filling the jar with one cup of water. Add a pinch of a colour to the water and stir it. Pour the oil into the jar. Secure the lid of the jar and shake it for 10 to 15 seconds. Keep the jar down and watch the liquid for a minute or two. After a while, add 1 to 2 teaspoons of the liquid dish soap and shake it again.

Skilling Up

Inquiry based

21ST CENTURY SKILLS

In the olden days, people drank water straight out of a tap. However, we always ask for bottled water. Find out how water is purified. Ask your science teacher what would happen if we drank saline water.

Extracting Groundwater

Rainwater not only fills ponds and lakes but is absorbed into the ground to form an underground reserve of water. Human beings use this groundwater for irrigation, drinking purposes and other **domestic** needs.

Many homes in villages have their own wells. Some villages have a common well for all the people. Water is drawn from the well using a pulley system. A **pulley** is a small wheel over which a rope is pulled to help lift heavy weights.

Pulley

domestic: for the house

Ancient sources of water

Many years ago, kings and queens built stepwells or *baolis* to ensure that water was available in the kingdom throughout the year, even during periods of drought. Stepwells date back to ancient India. These are storage tanks built deep into the ground for storing rainwater. The sides of the tanks are made of beautifully carved stones. Baolis or stepwells had steps that went all the way down so that people could collect the water. **Agrasen ki Baoli** in New Delhi is a famous stepwell. Baolis also provided shelter from the hot summer sun.

Agrasen ki Baoli

Matter of Fact

Plastic bottles take many years to decompose and damage the environment. Therefore, scientists have created edible water bottles called Ooho. Their outer covering is made of seaweed which is both edible and biodegradable.

Piaaos originally were wells dug along highways for long-distance travellers. Nowadays, piaaos are earthenware pots, either kept along the roadsides or dug into the mud along roads to keep the water cool. Modern-day piaaos have water taps attached to a tiled structure. People can drink this water for free. These are usually maintained by the government, religious or **charitable** organisations.

Water for Irrigation

In India, agriculture is the primary occupation. Different crops are grown in different regions of the country depending on the rainfall received. Crops require a constant supply of water to grow well. Traditionally, farmers in India relied heavily on rainwater. They also used water from wells to manually irrigate their fields. Tube wells, canals and tanks are some of the traditional sources of water used for irrigation.

Irrigation canal

Tube wells and **wells** are deep holes dug in the ground to draw groundwater. Water is manually drawn from a well by a bucket and rope. Nowadays, an electric pump is used to draw water from deep wells. These are called tube wells. In order to irrigate fields, this water is poured into channels dug between the rows of crops in the fields.

charitable: helping people who are poor or in need

Canals are channels made for irrigation from a large tank where rainwater is stored. In villages, canals leading from rivers and ponds carry water to the fields.

A **waterwheel** is a large wheel with buckets that is used for drawing water. It is driven by flowing water. As each bucket fills with water, it becomes heavy and pulls the wheel downward. This helps the wheel turn around, causing water in the bucket to be emptied on the other side in the channel that is made to irrigate the field. Animals are also used to draw the water. Waterwheels are also used to grind corn and wheat to flour as well as to generate energy.

Waterwheel

Smart Skills

Life skills

21ST CENTURY SKILLS

Reduce, **Reuse** and **Recycle** is the mantra to conserve water.
In groups, prepare a chart about how you can use water judiciously at your homes and school. Make a PowerPoint presentation that depicts reducing water usage, reusing wastewater, and recycling used water. Share your presentation with the others in the class.

Water Scarcity

Even today, many men and women have to walk miles to fetch water. Can you imagine how many rounds they make to fetch water for an entire household?

Water is one of the most important natural resource on Earth. Unfortunately, it is becoming **scarce**. As the population continues to grow, the demand for water is increasing. Washing clothes, bathing animals and throwing garbage and factory waste in rivers pollute the water sources. Thus, we are facing a scarcity of clean drinking water.

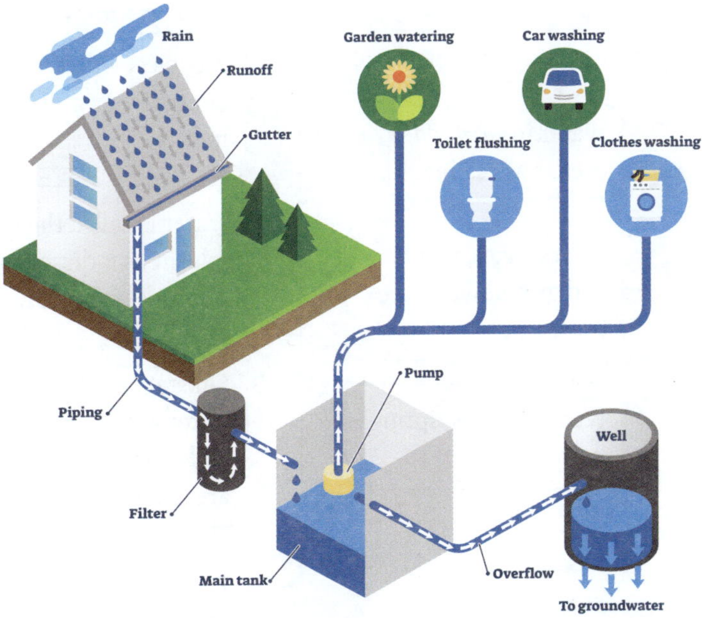

Rainwater harvesting

We need to conserve water so that we do not run out of it. We can save water by taking bucket baths, closing the taps when not in use and fixing leaking pipes. **Rainwater harvesting** is a method that helps conserve and restore groundwater levels.

scarce: too little, not enough

Smart Skills

Information literacy

Interview the people who help you at home or at school. You can ask your grandparents the same questions too.

- For what purposes do you use water?
- Do you get water throughout the day or only during fixed hours?
- Who gets up to collect and store the water?
- Do you drink water directly from a tap or do you boil/filter it first?
- How much do you have to travel to get water?
- Can you use the water freely or judiciously?
- Compare the answers. What did you observe?

What We Learnt

Water

- **Sources of water**
  - Water in seas and oceans are saline.
  - Rivers, lakes, ponds and groundwater are freshwater.
  - Water in wells, springs is groundwater.
    - Piaaos provide free drinking water to people.
- **Properties of Water**
  - An object will float if it is less dense than water, when placed in it.
  - Water is called the universal solvent as it dissolves more substances than any other liquid.
  - Substances that dissolve in water are soluble substances and those that do not dissolve are insoluble substances.
  - Water and oil never mix.
- **Uses**
  - Water is essential for growing crops and farmers irrigate their fields using tube wells and waterwheels.
  - Water is essential for all living things.

Think and Answer

A. Fill in the blanks.

1. Hot springs are formed when .... (well/groundwater/ponds) gets heated.
2. .... (salt/chalk/sugar) do not dissolve in water.
3. Liquid in which solute is dissolved is known as .... (solute/soluble/solvent).
4. .... (Canals/wells/ponds) are deep holes dug in the ground to draw out groundwater.
5. Only .... (1 percent/3 percent/4 percent) of the water on the Earth is fit for drinking.

B. Define the following terms.

1. Baoli
2. Piaao
3. Tube wells

C. Match the following.

1. Saline water	a. Irrigation
2. Water table	b. Seas
3. Solubility	c. Floats on water
4. Oil	d. Top level of groundwater
5. Canals	e. Ability to dissolve

D. Write *T* for true and *F* for false.

1. Water is precious and we must use it wisely. ☐
2. A piaao is a source of groundwater. ☐
3. Rainwater harvesting can be done at home. ☐
4. Waterwheels make it easy for farmers to irrigate their fields. ☐
5. In manual irrigation, water is drawn from wells and poured into the fields. ☐

E. Answer these questions.

1. Differentiate between underground and surface water.
2. What is a waterwheel?
3. How does the traditional irrigation system work?
4. What is the water table? How do we obtain underground water?
5. What is water scarcity?

Cross Connect

Marble art on paper

Materials required

Two to three coloured acrylic paints, water, oil, dropper, paintbrushes, a sheet of paper (cut in such a way that it fits in the container), water container large enough for the paper to fit in,

Method

- Take the container and pour water so that one-third of the container is full.
- Add drops of oil on the water using the dropper (about 1 1/2 teaspoon of oil).
- Dilute your paints a little.
- Tap your paintbrush on the container so that the paint splatters on water.
- Once the whole surface is covered with paints use the toothpick to make designs on the floating colours.
- Once done take the paper and float it on the surface of water. The pattern will form on the paper. Hold the corners to pick it up and let it dry. A beautiful marble painting will form on the paper.

Web link

For more information, log on to:
https://kids.nationalgeographic.com/5-reasons-why/article/5-reasons-why-water-rules

Last accessed on 30 August 2021

Unit 5: Shelter

15. Living Together

Get Going

Social Insects

Myra and Diya were turning pages of a book named *Insects*. Suddenly, they came across a sentence, 'Some insects are called social insects because they live in some highly organised societies.' 'What! They live in a society like us?' asked Diya. Both were surprised and curious when mother told them that almost all animals live in a group.

- Do you know of any insects that live in groups? Name them.
- Discuss why they live in a group.
- Name some animals who live in groups.

Like humans, some animals live in groups. They do so to protect themselves, to collect food and to take care of their young ones. Some animals live in small groups, while others live in large groups. When animals of the same species interact with each other, they **exhibit** **social behaviour**. Some insects too live together in **colonies**. They interact with each other, work together and depend on each other. They are called **social insects**. Ants, bees and termites are some social insects.

Picture Study

Why do some animals live in groups and some do not?

Ants

An **ant colony** is a group of ants that lives together underground, in trees or even inside plants. An ant colony is built by **worker ants** who spend their time digging tunnels. They carry fine soil, sand or clay and deposit it on a surface, forming an **anthill**.

exhibit: to show a quality, or a behaviour

These colonies are of different types. Some are simple mounds while others are made up of several chambers connected by tunnels. Different chambers are used for different purposes: for laying eggs, for nursing the larvae, for storing food and for resting.

Inside an anthill

Ants work together

In each ant colony, there is one **queen ant**, many male ants and many female worker ants. Some colonies are made up of millions of ants. The work is divided among the members of the colony. The queen ant lays eggs, the male ants help to reproduce and worker ants build and repair the colony and take care of the queen and the young ants. Some worker ants defend their colony from their enemies and are called **army ants**. Ants are very loyal to their colony and do not welcome outsiders. Ants of a colony often compete with other ants for food.

Matter of Fact

Ants are one of the world's strongest creatures in comparison to their size. A single ant can carry fifty times its own body weight. Ants even work together as a group to move bigger objects.

Skilling Up — Life skills — 21ST CENTURY SKILLS

- Have you ever seen ants walking in a line?
- What happens when you break this line?
- What effect does turmeric powder have on ants?

Communication

The members of an ant colony communicate with each other to manage and organize their activities. They use a special chemical to communicate with each other. They smell it with their antennae. The workers release a trail of special substances or scents that instruct the others to follow or attack them. In addition, ants also use touch and vibration to communicate in some situations.

Honeybees

Like ants, honeybees are also social insects. They live together in an enclosed structure called a **beehive** in which honeybees raise their young ones. Therefore, a beehive is a nest where a colony of bees live. It is built from the wax that the bees produce. A beehive consists of several **compartments**. These compartments are **hexagonal** in shape. These are used for laying eggs and storing pollen grains and honey. All these compartments together make up a **honeycomb**.

Beehive

Smart Skills

Problem-solving

21ST CENTURY SKILLS

- Bees are usually attracted to wide, open, and brightly coloured flowers, or sweet-scented flowers. Think why.
- What will happen if bees become extinct? Discuss.

Honeybees work together

A beehive usually consists of a single **queen bee**, many male bees or **drones** and female bees or **workers**. The queen bee, whose main job is to lay eggs, is the largest bee in the hive. She can lay a thousand or more eggs per day. Before laying eggs, she inspects each cell to ensure it has been cleaned by the workers.

The drones help the queen bee to reproduce. They are shorter than the queen and larger than the workers. Drones rarely feed themselves, instead, they hold out their tongues and a worker bee places food on it. The worker bees are responsible for collecting nectar, feeding and taking care of the young ones. They clean the hive and guard it.

Give It a Shot

E

- Name two animals and birds which live in a group and write one interesting fact about them.
- Name two animals which do not live in a group.

Smart Skills

Digital literacy

21ST CENTURY SKILLS

Find out how honeybees are important to the environment. Research on how honeybees help in pollination. In groups of four make a PowerPoint presentation.

Communication

Honeybees cannot talk to each other, so they communicate through dances, vibrations and smells. Once they find new pollen, nectar and water sources, honeybees return to the hive

Round dance

Waggle dance

compartments: separate sections; **hexagonal:** having six straight sides and six angles

and perform certain dances near it. The **round dance** is performed when the food source is within a hundred metres of the hive. The **waggle dance** is performed if the source is further away. To indicate distance, worker bees use an **audible** code of buzzes.

Smart Skills

Information literacy

21ST CENTURY SKILLS

Let us do a project on 'social behaviour of insects and what they teach us.' Besides ants and honeybees, termites and wasps also exhibit social behaviour. Find out how they live and communicate and what we can learn from them. Prepare a scrapbook and paste pictures in it.

What We Learnt

- Social Animals
  - Some of things that we can learn from social animals are sharing, caring, cooperation and division of labour.
  - Insects that live together in colonies, interact with each other, work together, and depend on each other are called social insects.
  - Ants
    - An ant colony is a home for ants which is usually underground and made up of several chambers connected by tunnels.
  - Ants and bees have a special way of communicating with members of the ant colony and the beehive.
  - Bees
    - A beehive is an enclosed structure in which honeybees live and raise their young ones.

Think and Answer

A. Fill in the blanks with the correct answers.

1. Worker ants carry fine soil, sand or clay and deposit it on a surface, forming an ....

   a. tunnel b. anthill c. ant colony

round dance: where dancers move in a circle; **waggle dance:** a series of figure-eight movements performed by a bee to indicate the direction and abundance of a distant food source; **audible:** a sound that can be heard clearly

2. .... help the queen bee to reproduce.

a. Drones b. Worker bees c. Worker ants

3. A .... is a nest where a colony of bee lives.

a. compartment b. beehive c. tunnel

4. An ant smells with the help of its.............................. .

a. skin b. nose c. antenna

5. A .... bee collects nectar.

a. honey b. worker c. drone

B. Define the following.

1. Social behaviour
2. Beehive
3. Honeycomb
4. Drones
5. Waggle dance

C. Fill in the blanks.

1. Honeybees perform the waggle dance when the new pollen, nectar and water source is .... away.
2. ...., ... and .... are social insects.
3. Ants carry fine dust particles and deposit them to form an.............................. .
4. The compartments in a beehive together form a.............................. .
5. Ants also use touch and vibration to .... in some situations.

D. Write *T* for true and *F* for false.

1. The queen bee takes care of the young ones. ☐
2. Male ants defend their colonies from enemies. ☐
3. Honeybees communicate through dances, vibrations and chemicals. ☐
4. Ants cannot communicate with their antennae. ☐
5. Worker ants who defend their colony from their enemies are called army ants. ☐

E. Answer these questions.

1. Why do some animals live in groups?
2. What do you understand by the term 'social insects'?
3. Define the terms ant colony, anthill and beehive.
4. Explain the role played by various ants in an ant colony.
5. How do honeybees work together?

Cross Connect

Dance Like a Bee

- Try doing the waggle dance of honeybees and learn the correct way to do the round dance.

Number of players: 16 to 20.

Divide the class into two teams.

- Each team should form a long line, holding hands, facing the other team. The two teams should be around 20 or so feet apart. The teams take turn calling out , 'Red Rover, Red Rover, let us come over!'
- One student leaves their team's line, runs as fast as he or she can towards the other line and tries to break through the held hands.
- If through, they get to take someone back to their team. If they do not, they join the new team.
- When a team only has one person left, that person tries to break through the other team. If they do not, then their team loses. If they do, they gain a player and the game continues.

Web link

For more information, log on to:
https://kids.nationalgeographic.com/animals/mammals/facts/african-elephant

Last accessed on 30 August 2021

16. Our Surroundings

Unit 5: Shelter

Get Going

Shelter and a place to live has been a basic need of human beings since the time of early humans. However, as you have learnt, humans did not always live in the kind of houses we see around us today. The concept of settlement and living with others around us started once humans learnt to grow food. Over the centuries, the kinds of houses or shelters built by humans has also changed and developed.

Look at the pictures given below and put them in order from the time of early humans to today by numbering them.

People who live next to and near our houses are our **neighbours**. Our neighbours and their homes together make a **neighbourhood** or a colony. Villages, towns and cities are made of several neighbourhoods. The villages are called rural areas and the towns and cities called urban areas. Every urban neighbourhood has common **facilities** like parks, schools, hospitals and parking spaces for vehicles. Interacting with and helping our neighbours make the neighbourhood a friendly and safe place.

facilities: a place, amenity or an equipment provided for a particular purpose

When you walk around your neighbourhood, do all the buildings look alike? Buildings and houses of different styles are found in a neighbourhood. People build houses of different designs and structures depending on the climatic conditions, the locally available materials and the cost.

Smart Skills — Design thinking — 21ST CENTURY SKILLS

How do you imagine a smart neighbourhood should look like? In groups, design your modern, smart neighbourhood and mention how you can make it environmentally friendly. Make a PowerPoint presentation or a video and present to the class.

Climatic Conditions

Climate and geographical features of a region determine the design and structure of a house.

Houses in the plains have **flat roofs**. Hot regions with extreme weather during summer and winter have houses with thick walls and high ceilings. This helps in keeping the houses cool in the summer and warm in the winter. Windows and **ventilators** allow the warm air to go out and cool air to enter.

Houses in plains

Smart Skills — Information literacy — 21ST CENTURY SKILLS

Houses with flat roofs can also be found very high up in the mountains. Find out the name of the state or the union territory of India which is high in the mountains in the north but has flat-roof houses. What geographical and climate conditions are behind building such houses?

Houses in mountains and hilly areas that receive heavy snowfall have **sloping roofs** that allow the snow to slide off the roof preventing the house from becoming cold and **damp**. Their walls and the floor are usually made of wood as it keeps the house warm.

Houses built in regions that receive heavy rainfall also have sloping roofs. Areas that are prone to floods have houses built on **stilts**. In India, we can find these kinds of houses in Arunachal Pradesh.

Houses in hilly regions

ventilators: a device or an opening for letting fresh air come into a room; **damp:** wet; **stilts:** upright poles that support a building

Tents are temporary and mobile houses that protect from rain, harsh sunlight and sandstorms. Early humans lived in tents much before they learnt how to build houses. Many thousands of years later, the native Americans also called Red Indians, lived in tents. Do you know what their tents were called? Nomads and gypsies, who carry their homes with them, use tents as houses as they can be folded and moved easily.

Matter of Fact

The nomads of Mongolia, Siberia and Turkey live in a circular tent called **yurt**. It is made of **felt** and bamboo sticks.

In countries like Japan, where earthquakes are common, people live in traditional houses made of bamboo and wood. These materials are light and do not cause severe injuries if they collapse during an earthquake.

Smart Skills — Life Skills — 21ST CENTURY SKILLS

Imagine that you have planned to go on a camping trip with your family this summer vacation. Make a list of all the items you will carry with you for the trip. Remember that on a camping trip, you will have to carry your belongings by yourself. You are allowed only ten items. Make a list of things you would like to take with you.

Building Materials

People mostly use locally available materials to build their houses. In villages, mud, straw and wood are easily available, so these are the primary materials for building houses. Such houses are not structurally strong and often get destroyed by strong winds and heavy rainfall and need to be repaired. These are called **kutcha houses**.

Kutcha house

Some villages have big houses called havelis, which are built by the **zamindar** or the land owner of the village. Havelis are expensive and high-cost houses.

Houses built with materials like bricks, cement and iron are strong and can withstand harsh weather conditions are called **pucca houses**. We find such houses in towns and cities. Nowadays, these materials are easily available even in villages and so, many village houses are also pucca houses.

Pucca house

Tall buildings are being built in big cities due to the lack of space. These buildings are called multi-storeyed buildings or high rises.

felt: a smooth cloth made of wool and other textiles

Cost of Building Houses

Neighbourhoods in cities have a mix of small and big houses, such as huge bungalows, small apartments and multi-storeyed high rises. Houses vary in size and design depending on how much a person can spend on the construction or buying of the house.

Apartment complex

Cities have low-cost houses too. They are called **chawls** and provide basic accommodation to people. Chawls are multi-storeyed buildings divided into several one-room or two-room living units. Chawls are mostly found in Maharashtra in India.

Chawl

People who leave their homes in villages to find work in the city have little money to find or build a house for themselves. Many of them live on the streets or build **makeshift** houses. Some areas in cities have tightly packed temporary houses made of materials like tin, plastic or plywood. These areas are called **slums**.

Sharing Resources

A good neighbour is one who is friendly, **considerate** and respects your space and privacy. However, to have a good neighbour, we have to first become good neighbours ourselves.

Give It a Shot

E

Read the names of the different types of houses. In your notebook, write the names of the states where these houses are found.

houseboat   stilt houses   houses with sloping roof   flat roof houses   high rises   chawls

We have learnt earlier that a neighbourhood has common **amenities** like water, electricity, road and park. These are shared and used by everyone. We need to be considerate and **judicious** in using them so that there is enough for all. To be good neighbours, we must be understanding, helpful, kind and respectful towards our neighbours. Being a good neighbour develops a sense of community and belonging.

makeshift: used temporarily for a particular purpose because the real thing is not available; **considerate:** thinking of other people's wishes and feelings; **amenities:** a feature or service that makes a place pleasant; **judicious:** using good judgment and sense

Skilling Up

Critical thinking

Name any two resources that you share with your neighbour. These icons are given to you as clues. Write yes below the icon in case you share any of these. In your notebook, write two ways in which you use these resources judiciously.

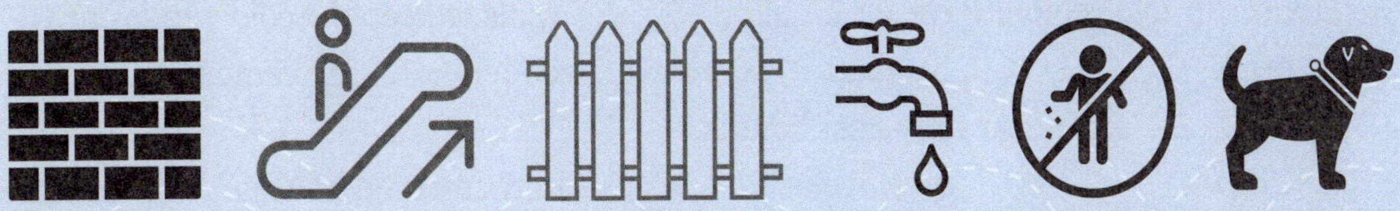

....

What We Learnt

Climatic Conditions
- People build different kinds of houses depending on the geographical region, climatic conditions, availability of building material and cost. Houses are usually built using locally available building materials.

Types of Houses
- Kutcha houses and pucca houses
- Pucca houses can be small or big, low-cost or expensive.

Neighbourhoods
- Our neighbours and their homes.
- Living together gives people a sense of community and belonging.
- People in a neighbourhood should share common facilities and use them judiciously.

Think and Answer

A. Fill in the blanks.

1. A good .... is a blessing.
2. We must show .... to our neighbours.
3. In places with hot climate, ... and .... are important for the circulation of air.
4. Neighbours are important because people .... on each other in times of need.
5. A haveli is a .... house.

B. Fill in the blanks with the correct answers.

1. In places that receive heavy snowfall, houses have .... roofs.
   a. flat b. sloping c. circular d. pointed
2. Tents are....................................... houses used by nomads.
   a. strong b. temporary c. kutcha d. big
3. Houses in cold regions have .... walls to keep the cold winds out.
   a. brick b. glass c. wooden d. cemented
4. .... are low-cost houses.
   a. Chawls b. Havelis c. Multi-storeyed houses d. Bungalows
5. We should be .... towards our neighbours.
   a. respectful b. disrespectful c. bad d. rude

C. Write *T* for true and *F* for false.

1. People in a neighbourhood should share resources. ☐
2. A good neighbourhood is one in which people do not talk to each other. ☐
3. In hot areas, houses are built on stilts. ☐
4. Nomads live in tents because they can be moved easily. ☐
5. Kutcha houses are found only in big cities. ☐

D. Answer these questions.

1. Name the factors that determine the kind of houses people build.
2. Differentiate between kutcha and pucca houses.
3. Why do houses in areas prone to floods have stilts?
4. What are some of the basic facilities that a neighbourhood needs?
5. How can we be good neighbours?

Cross Connect

Adventure Trip

Imagine you and your team are on an adventure trip to the desert of Rajasthan with your school friends. On arriving to the sand dunes, you are informed that a sandstorm will strike in 30 minutes. Working in groups make your shelter using only playing cards, rubber bands and sticky notes. Once ready, switch on the fan (ceiling fan or table fan) to check if your shelter can withstand the wind speed of the storm.

Web link

For more information, log on to:
https://www.re-thinkingthefuture.com/rtf-fresh-perspectives/a1537-evolution-of-housing-in-india/

Last accessed on 30 August 2021

17. Calamities

Unit 5: Shelter

Get Going

It was January 2020 when all of us and the entire world first heard of a new disease—the **coronavirus disease** or **COVID-19**. At that time no one imagined the extent of the crisis. The virus that causes this respiratory disease is called the coronavirus or SARS-CoV-2. It was first identified in December 2019 in Wuhan, China. A similar crisis called the Spanish Flu had occurred 100 years ago in the year 1919.

In March, the World Health Organization (WHO) declared a **Public Health Emergency**, and many countries along with India went into what none of us have experienced before—a lockdown. Everything closed for weeks all over India including trains, flights, restaurants, cinemas, even schools. People had to work from home. For students, their device became their school. Words like **masks, personal protective equipment (PPE)**, **containment zones** and **social distancing** that were hardly used or heard of became commonplace.

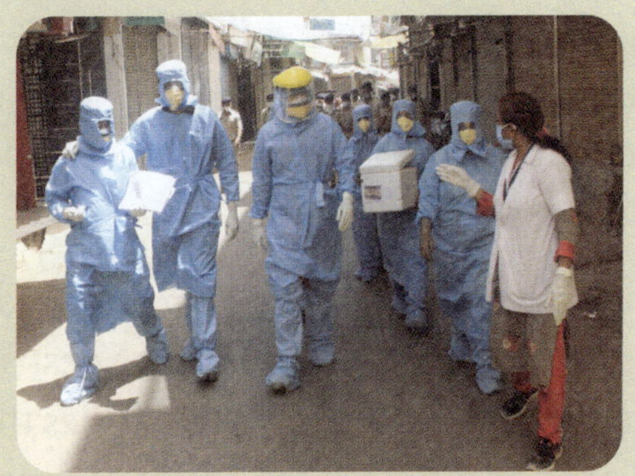

Covid-19 health team in Ahmedabad, India

Difficult situations and moments of emergency often come by surprise. A sudden accident or a natural **catastrophe** that causes great damage to property and loss of life is called a **disaster** or a **calamity**. It causes immense suffering and lasting **distress** to people and animals. Disasters can be natural or man-made. Earthquakes, tsunamis, cyclones, floods, volcanic eruptions and forest fires are some **natural disasters**.

Natural disasters are caused by forces of nature that are not within our control. Therefore, it is important that we are well-prepared to face them by learning about their causes, effects and how to deal with them.

catastrophe: an unexpected event that causes great suffering or damage; **distress:** extreme pain and suffering

Smart Skills

SEL

Recently, you, your family and people all over the world have lived through a calamity. What is this calamity called? It caused immense distress and suffering to a lot of people everywhere.

- What were some of the moments you found particularly difficult during this time?
- Were there any happy moments you experienced? What were these?

Make two cards one with a smiling face and another with a sad face. During **circle time** talk about your difficult and happy moments by holding up the appropriate card.

Earthquake

A sudden, violent shaking of the ground is called an **earthquake**. There are plates or blocks under the surface of the Earth that keep moving and shifting. On these plates lie the continents and the oceans. When these plates collide or slip over one another, there is a sudden release of energy which causes an earthquake.

Destruction caused by an earthquake

Earthquakes are difficult to predict and impossible to stop. They can cause immense destruction. The tremor of the earthquake shakes the buildings and houses. Some of these buildings collapse, resulting in the deaths of people and animals. Thus, many people become homeless. In hilly areas, earthquakes can cause **landslides**. Depending on the magnitude of the earthquake, bridges and dams too can crack or collapse which, in turn, causes floods.

The magnitude and intensity of an earthquake is measured by an instrument called a **seismometer**. Earthquakes also cause loss of electricity and breakdown of communication.

During an earthquake we should:

- Try to stay calm and not panic.
- Move to an open area that is away from buildings, trees and electric poles.
- Crouch under a heavy table or bed that can protect us from the falling **rubble** in case we can't get out of the building.

rubble: the pieces of brick, stone, or other materials that remain or fall when a building is destroyed

Give It a Shot

E

Mock earthquake drill in class

Remember to stay away from windows and glass. At the sound of the bell, get under the desks and perform the 'drop, cover and hold' step until the shaking stops.

Once the shaking stops, leave the building in a calm and orderly manner. Use your school bags to protect your head if enough desks are not available, or when there are no desks at all. Make sure not to run during an earthquake.

Learn the evacuation route from your class. Once you are out, stand in a line while the teachers do a body count of the students present.

Tsunami

Destruction caused by a tsunami

Tsunamis are giant ocean waves that are caused by severe earthquakes or volcanic eruptions that occur under the oceans. Huge waves of massive force lash the coastal areas, causing damage to life and property. The point on the earth that is straight above the point of origin of the earthquake deep in the ocean is called the **epicenter**. The earthquake spreads on Earth from this point.

In 2004, a huge tsunami originating in the Indian Ocean, hit the coast of Tamil Nadu, causing immense destruction and loss of life. The tsunami waves affected not just India, but also other countries located off the Indian Ocean. Indira Point, the southernmost point of India, was **submerged** due to the tsunami.

Skilling Up

Data analytics — 21ST CENTURY SKILLS

The tsunami that started in the Indian Ocean in 2004 impacted several countries including India. On a world map, colour the severely impacted and less severely impacted countries in different colours.

Severely impacted countries: India, Indonesia, Maldives, Sri Lanka, Thailand, Malaysia, Somalia, Myanmar

Less severely impacted countries: Kenya, South Africa, Tanzania, Madagascar, Seychelles

Looking at the countries you have coloured, can you think of a reason why the tsunami caused more damage in some countries than others?

submerged: to go under the surface of water

Cyclone

Cyclones are violent storms that cause strong winds and heavy rainfall. They are common in coastal areas and islands. The force and speed of the wind can uproot trees and electric poles and destroy buildings and bridges. The heavy rainfall also causes floods that destroys crops and endangers the lives of fishermen. The flood contaminates the water sources of the city spreading diseases.

Matter of Fact

India is amongst the worst affected countries in the world when it comes to cyclones. Majority of the cyclones in India emerge from the Bay of Bengal and hit the eastern coast of India with Andhra Pradesh and Odisha being the worst hit. Fewer cyclones emerge from the Arabian Sea.

Cyclone Ockhi hit the coastal areas of Kerala in 2017.

In the year 2020, **Cyclone Amphan** emerging from the Bay of Bengal, caused destruction in West Bengal and Odisha. **Cyclone Nisarga** emerged from the Arabian Sea and hit Alibag in Maharashtra.

Cyclone Yaas and **Cyclone Taukte** hit India in 2021.

Flooding caused by Cyclone Amphan

In the event of a cyclone or a tsunami, we should:

- Move to higher areas or stay indoors.
- Always keep an emergency kit containing medicines, torch, batteries and a waterproof bag.

Flood

Heavy rainfall causes the water in the rivers to overflow and **breach** the riverbanks. This overflow floods the adjoining areas, submerging roads and houses. Sometimes, bridges are also washed away, and communication becomes difficult. Crops are destroyed and people and animals die due to drowning. Diseases spread due to contamination caused by floodwater.

In 2014, Jammu and Kashmir faced severe floods that submerged many villages. More recently in 2020 during the pandemic, Assam faced floods causing destruction and distress to the people. The

Smart Skills

Digital literacy and Data collection

21ST CENTURY SKILLS

India faces devastating floods every year. Make a list of the floods in India in the last 10 years, the states in which these floods occurred and the destruction the floods caused. Make a PowerPoint presentation and present it in the class.

breach: an opening that is created by strong winds or seas

floods were caused due to unusually high monsoon rainfall and the overflowing of the Brahmaputra river in Assam.

In case of a flood, we should:

- Move to higher areas like the roof of a building or treetops.
- Spread the message so that everyone can prepare for safety measures or an evacuation.
- Keep an emergency kit with medicines in a waterproof bag with clothes, food and bottled water.
- Drink boiled or bottled water only.

Managing Disasters

Disasters can cause mental and physical **trauma** to survivors. People who survive disasters often face loss of family members, relatives or property. At such times, help from the community is important. Rescuing people buried under collapsed buildings, setting up emergency relief shelters and camps for the survivors to stay, providing first aid, food and clean drinking water and many other things are needed in the **aftermath** of a disaster.

Many governmental and non-governmental organizations (NGOs) and charitable groups help people that are affected by a disaster.

- Organisations such as the Indian Red Cross Society (IRCS) and the United Nations also carry out rescue and relief operations.
- Citizens help by donating money, food, medicines and clothes. They also help by donating blood, transporting relief supplies and **volunteering** in the affected areas.
- Emergency services are provided by the police, the fire department and hospitals. The police help by maintaining law and order and taking the rescued people to relief camps.
- Doctors and nurses and other healthcare workers play an important role in rescue operations.
- The army also engages in rescue and relief operations. They clear rubble from the roads and distribute food and medicines.

Rescue team helping people

trauma: severe shock; **aftermath:** a situation that exists after an event; **volunteer:** to do some task for free

We too can help

Here are some of the ways we can help others before, during and after a disaster.

- Collect clothes, medicines and other items as required for the people trapped in affected areas.
- Remind people to take cover under heavy tables or help them move to open areas during an earthquake or on rooftops during a flood.
- Call a doctor in case of an emergency. When calling for medical help, be sure to provide clear information and the exact location.
- Give first aid to the injured.

Smart Skills Life skills 21ST CENTURY SKILLS

- If you could volunteer to be a part of an NGO, how would you like to help and why?
- Why should we not to enter a building soon after an earthquake?
- Why should we move to higher areas during floods?

Providing First Aid

First aid is the immediate help provided to an injured person before a doctor or medical help arrives. If given on time, it can prevent the injured person's condition from becoming worse and even save his or her life.

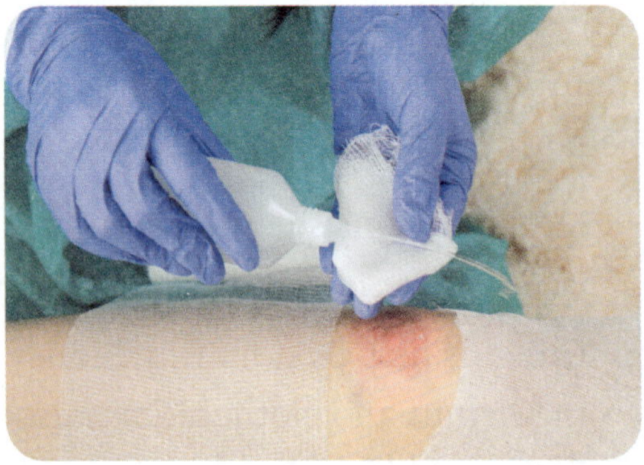
Covering a wound

Cuts and wounds: Wash hands with soap and water. Clean the bleeding wound with an antiseptic lotion and then cover it with a medicated tape, cotton pad or a bandage. In case the blood flow is still heavy, raise the wounded body part above the level of the heart to slow down the blood flow from the wound.

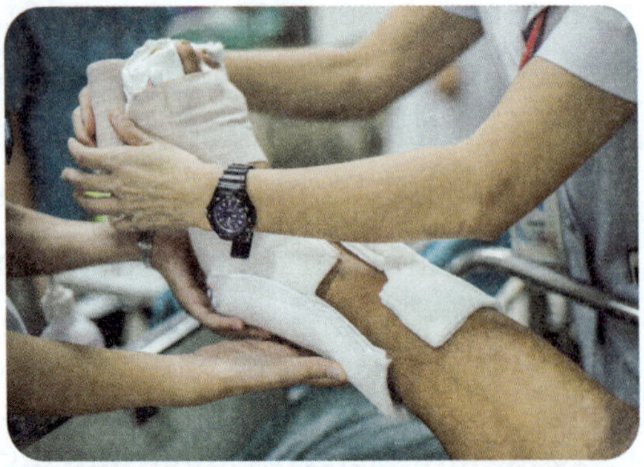
Splinting

Fracture: A fracture is a broken bone. We must not move the broken part of the body. Gently attach a **splint** to support the broken bone and prevent its movement. A splint can be a long piece of wood, cardboard, a measuring scale or even a folded newspaper. In case of fracture in the arm, after

splint: a long piece of wood or metal that is tied to a broken arm or leg to keep it still and in the right position

tying the splint, put the arm in a sling for support. The patient should then be taken to a doctor immediately.

Sprain: A sprain is an injury caused by sudden twisting of a joint. It can cause pain or swelling. Use an ice pack on the sprain to reduce the swelling. Apply pain-relieving ointment on the injury and tie a crepe bandage around the sprained area to prevent the movement of the joint.

Fainting: A person who has fainted should be laid down on his or her back. In case there are no injuries and the person is breathing, we should raise his or her legs above the heart level. Loosen the collar, belts or any other tight clothing that the person may be wearing. Do not crowd around the person, so that he or she gets enough air to breathe.

It is important to have a first aid kit with essential medical items for treating common injuries such as wounds, fractures and sprains. We should also always carry a first aid kit with us with essential medicines while travelling.

Picture Study

Your friend falls and cuts his knee while playing football in a park near your house. You bring your friend home, but your parents are not there. Look at the picture and say what first aid will you give your friend to stop the bleeding.

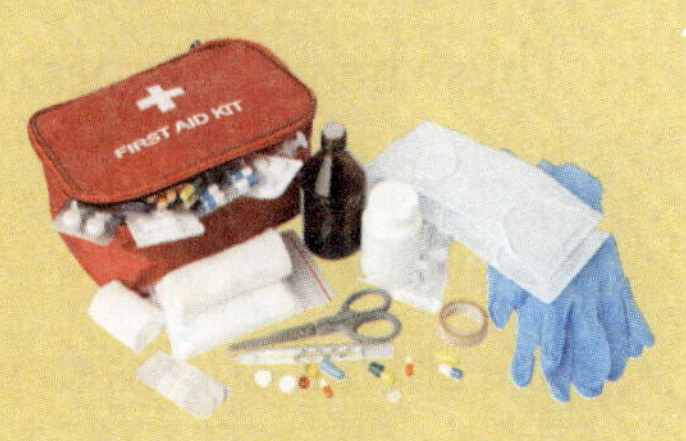

What We Learnt

Disasters or calamties occur suddenly and cause destruction of life and property. These can be natural or man-made.

Earthquakes, tsunamis, floods, cyclones, forest fires and volcanic eruptions are forms of natural disasters.

The army, police, hospitals, NGOs and international organisations provide help and relief in the aftermath of a disaster.

We too can provide help and support in many simple ways to the survivors of disasters.

First aid is the immediate help given to an injured person before a doctor or medical help arrives. We should always carry a first aid kit with essential medicines while travelling.

Think and Answer

A. Fill in the blanks.

1. Natural disasters are caused by the forces of ....
2. The .... helps us to measure the strength of an earthquake.
3. .... is the immediate help given to an injured person.
4. Violent storms that bring strong winds and heavy rainfall are called ....
5. A natural disaster affects both .... and ....
6. A broken bone is called a ....

B. Tick the correct answers.

1. Tsunamis are caused by
   a. Heavy rainfall
   b. Overflowing rivers
   c. Earthquakes under the ocean
   d. All of them
2. Cyclones in India mostly emerge more from the
   a. Arabian Sea
   b. Indian Ocean
   c. Bay of Bengal
   d. River Ganga
3. These help survivors of disasters
   a. Red Cross
   b. United Nations
   c. NGOs
   d. All of them
4. We should do this to protect ourselves during an earthquake
   a. Stand near a window
   b. Run
   c. Get under heavy tables
   d. Stand under doorways
5. When someone faints, we should
   a. Quickly make the person sit
   b. Crowd around the person
   c. Tie a belt tightly around them
   d. Raise their legs above their heart

C. Match the columns.

1. Tsunami	a. Injury caused by twisting a joint
2. Floods	b. Rescue operations
3. Sprain	c. Heavy rainfall
4. Army	d. Earthquake
5. Seismometer	e. Coast of Tamil Nadu

D. Answer these questions.

1. What are natural calamities? Give any two examples.
2. What is an earthquake? What should we do when an earthquake occurs?
3. How do floods affect the lives of the people?

4. What are the effects of a cyclone? What precautions should people take if a cyclone occurs?
5. What is a fracture? What first aid should be given in case of a fracture?

Cross Connect

HC CC

In groups make a list of the precautions to take during a pandemic. Also, think of how the tables and chairs can be placed in the class so that physical distancing can be maintained between the students, but all are facing the blackboard. Make a drawing or sketch on how your classroom should post-pandemic. Share your ideas with the entire class during **Show and Tell**.

Web link

For more information, log on to:
https://kids.nationalgeographic.com/science/article/hurricane

Last accessed on 30 August 2021

Unit 6: Travel

18. Fuels

Get Going

Look at the pictures and write the kind of fuel used by these vehicles, they may be more than one kind.

....

Abbreviations of two types of fuels are given below. Write their full forms.

ATF ....

HFO ....

A **fuel** is a source of energy. It produces energy when burnt. **Petrol**, **diesel**, **kerosene**, **coal**, **liquefied petroleum gas (LPG)** and **compressed natural gas (CNG)** are some fuels. They are used in vehicles, for cooking and for producing electricity. Some fuels are found naturally, while some are artificially produced or made by human beings.

Fossil Fuels

Coal, petroleum and natural gas are **fossil fuels**. They are formed from the remains of ancient plants and animals buried deep inside the Earth millions of years ago. Fossil fuels are **non-renewable** sources of energy. Therefore, they must be used **judiciously**.

Coal

Coal is found deep under the Earth's surface. It is a solid fossil fuel and is the largest source of energy on Earth. It is widely used to generate electricity. It is also used in factories for making iron and steel and other goods.

non-renewable: a natural resource that exists in limited supply and cannot be replaced; **judiciously:** to use something wisely

Skilling Up

Information Literacy

21ST CENTURY SKILLS

- What is the fuel used in ships called?
- Do all vehicles consume an equal amount of fuel?

Millions of years ago, the Earth was covered with damp forests in which plants such as giant ferns and mosses grew. Some of these plants died and fell into marshy land. New plants grew in their place and the cycle continued. **Gradually**, a thick layer of dead plants started forming on Earth. This process continued for years. Through millions of years, many layers of **decomposed** plants kept forming, one on top of the other, which changed into coal under heat and pressure.

Coal is obtained by digging deep inside the Earth. This is known as **coal mining**. Deep holes called **mines** are dug into the Earth's surface and coal is taken out using machines. In India, coal is found in Jharkhand, West Bengal, Odisha, Madhya Pradesh, Andhra Pradesh and Tamil Nadu. The major coal mines in India are in Bokaro, Dhanbad, Jharia, Raniganj and Korba. Coal was used in **angithis** to cook food and to keep homes warm during winter in the olden days.

Coal mine

Petroleum

Petroleum is a type of **crude** mineral oil. It is also known as 'black gold'. It is formed from the remains of plants and animals buried under the sea or land for millions of years. Petroleum is black in colour and has a distinct smell. Areas under the sea where petroleum is found are called **reservoirs**. It is taken out after drilling deep wells under the sea. The oil is refined in oil refineries and then processed into various products such as petrol, diesel, kerosene, LPG and paraffin wax.

Oil rig

Smart Skills

Critical thinking

21ST CENTURY SKILLS

How would your life be if there was no coal and petroleum in the world? List the things that you would not be able to do.

gradually: slowly; **decomposed:** when something decays or rots; **angithi:** a portable heater consisting of a pan or stand for holding lighted coals; **crude:** in a natural or raw state; **reservoir:** a large natural source

Petroleum reservoirs in India are found in Mumbai High Field, located off the coast of Mumbai, Digboi and Sivasagar in Assam, and Ankleshwar and Khambhat in Gujarat. Oil refineries in India are located in Mumbai, Haldia, Digboi, Kochi, Barauni, Chennai and Mathura.

Give It a Shot

E

Find out the cost of petrol or diesel per litre in your state or union territory and three neighbouring states.

State/Union Territory	Petrol	Diesel

Talk to your parents or grandparents about the cost of fuel when they were young.

Natural gas

Natural gas is found along with petroleum in oil wells. It is used as a domestic and industrial fuel. CNG is also used as a fuel for motor vehicles. It is considered a clean fuel as it does not cause pollution. It is cheaper than petrol and diesel. CNG can be supplied directly from gas fields through pipelines. Vadodara in Gujarat and some parts of the National Capital Region (NCR) have this network of pipelines.

Matter of Fact

Jatropha is a plant whose seeds are crushed, to produce jatropha oil which can be processed to produce a high- quality biodiesel. Biodiesel is used in a standard diesel car or further processed into jet fuel.

Vehicles Without Fuel

In earlier times, people would walk long distances. **Palanquins** were used to carry kings or queens from one place to another. Then came bicycles, rickshaws and vehicles like *tongas* and bullock carts. Rickshaws were drawn and cycles were ridden by humans to travel short distances. Tongas and bullock carts were drawn by animals to travel longer distances.

palanquin: a large box carried on two horizontal poles by four or six people

Uses of Fuels

Fuels are used for many purposes.

- Petrol is essential for transportation. It is used in cars, school buses, trucks and other vehicles.
- Diesel is widely used as fuel for vehicles such as tractors, trailer trucks, buses, boats and trains.
- LPG is an eco-friendly fuel used at home and in some vehicles.
- Coal is used as a fuel in factories. It is also used for generating electricity.
- CNG is used as a fuel for vehicles. It is especially used in public transport as it is cheaper.
- Kerosene is used as a fuel for cooking, lighting and heating.
- Paraffin wax, a **by-product** of petroleum, is used to make candles.

CNG filling station

Pollution by Fuels

Burning of fuel can produce energy and harmful substances that can be mixed in the air causing air pollution. When fossil fuels are burned, they release nitrogen oxides into the atmosphere, which contribute to the formation of smog and acid rain. This effects our health and can cause harm to plants and animals. Millions of Indians die every year from air pollution caused by burning fossil fuels.

Picture Study

- Look at the picture, do you agree with what the parents are saying? Why?
- How do you travel to school from home?

Conservation of Fuels

There is a limited supply of fossil fuels on Earth. Coal, petroleum and natural gas take millions of years to form. Therefore, conserving these fuels is very important.

by-product: a secondary product that is produced while manufacturing another product

Smart Skills

Life skills

21ST CENTURY SKILLS

7 AFFORDABLE AND CLEAN ENERGY

Pollution Under Control (PUC) is a certificate issued by the government of India to the owners of vehicles. This certificate implies that the vehicle is using fuel that does not pollute the environment.

- Why is it important to get pollution check of your vehicles?
- At what interval should you get your vehicles checked?
- What steps would you take to help the environment?

The following steps can be taken to conserve fuels.

- **Carpooling** means sharing rides with friends, family or even neighbours. Carpooling can help us conserve fuel.
- Using public transport and local trains instead of your own vehicles.
- Turning off the car engine when the car is not moving or at longer traffic signals.
- Using bicycles and rickshaws for travelling short distances instead of cars, scooters or motorcycles.
- Walking to nearby places instead of using cars or motorcycles not only reduces pollution but also reduces the amount of fuel used.
- Switching to electric vehicles instead of fuel vehicles as this will reduce pollution and help in creating clean environment.
- Scientists and researchers have invented and created **electric cars**. We can see electric cabs on the roads.

Electric car

Alternative Sources of Energy

There are many alternative sources of energy on Earth. We get solar energy from the Sun, **geothermal** energy from the Earth and wind energy from the wind. These are called renewable or alternative sources of energy as they are available to us in large quantities and can be **replenished**. By using these, we can conserve non-renewable resources of

geothermal: produced by the internal heat of the Earth; **replenish:** fill up again

energy. **Biogas** is produced from waste materials and used as a cooking fuel. Sunlight or solar energy can be used directly for heating and lighting homes, streets and other buildings, and heating water. It also has a variety of commercial and industrial uses.

Smart Skills

Life skills

21ST CENTURY SKILLS

In groups of four, prepare a PowerPoint presentation on ways to conserve fuel and energy and find different alternative sources of energy. Present it in front of the class.

What We Learnt

Fuels

- Fuels can be natural or man-made.
- Fuels are used in vehicles, for cooking and for producing electricity.
- Alternative sources of energy can be used to conserve non-renewable sources of energy.
- Coal, petroleum and natural gas are fossil fuels.
- Fossil fuels are natural fuels. They are formed from the remains of plants and animals that were buried under the Earth millions of years ago.
- Natural gas is also found along with petroleum. CNG is a clean fuel.
- Fossil fuels are non-renewable sources of energy and are present under the surface of the Earth in limited quantities.

Think and Answer

A. Answer in one word.

1. Fuels formed from the remains of ancient plants and animals ....
2. Digging coal out of the Earth ....
3. Crude mineral oil ....
4. A two-wheeled vehicle that runs without fuel ....
5. Sharing rides with friends, family or neighbours ....

B. Fill in the blanks with correct answer.

1. .... (wood/coal/stone) is a solid fossil fuel and is the largest source of energy.
2. Areas under the sea where petroleum is found are .... (refineries/reservoirs/ replenished).
3. .... (Rickshaws/Palanquins/Bullock carts) were used to carry kings or queens from one place to another.
4. In India, coal is found in .... (Delhi/Jharkhand/ Kashmir).
5. .... (Solar energy/Kerosene oil/Wind) is a renewable source of energy.

C. Write *T* for true and *F* for false.

1. Sunlight is a non-renewable source of energy. ☐
2. Oil refineries are located in Mumbai, Haldia, Digboi and Mathura. ☐
3. Biogas is produced from waste materials and used as cooking fuel. ☐
4. Coal is found deep inside the Earth and is known as 'black gold'. ☐
5. Kerosene cannot be used as a fuel. ☐

D. Answer these questions.

1. How is petroleum formed?
2. Name the major petroleum producing regions of India.
3. Name some vehicles that operate without fuel.
4. What are some of the methods of conserving energy?
5. What is an alternative source of energy?
6. Define non-renewable resources of energy and fossil fuels.

Cross Connect

HC CC

7 AFFORDABLE AND CLEAN ENERGY

- Hold a debate in class on the advantages and disadvantages of using alternative sources of energy.
- Draw, create and make an innovative vehicle of your imagination, which will work on alternative energy of your choice.

Web link

For more information, log on to:
https://www.nationalgeographic.org/article/renewable-energy/

Last accessed on 30 August 2021

Unit 6: Travel

19. Climb Every Mountain

Get Going

Adventure Sports

Have you been to Shimla, Manali or Mussoorie or any other hill station on a camping trip? When you are there you see mountains all around you. People are found having fun trying to climb these mountains or enjoy a ride on the river in rafts. You must have seen some people trying to cross the river by hanging on ropes. Wall climbing for children and paragliding are some other types of activities commonly found in these camps. These activities are sports that may be hard to do, but give a great thrill to those who try and can complete them. These sports activities are also known as adventure sports.

Mountaineering, river rafting, rock climbing and paragliding are adventure sports or adventure activities. Throughout the ages, humans have been fascinated by nature and find the experience of adventure sports thrilling. People enjoy the excitement of these daring activities. Their determination to succeed and spirit of adventure drives them to accomplish such feats.

Mountaineering

The sport or activity of climbing mountains is called **mountaineering**. The great Himalayas, 'the abode of snow', have always fascinated people. Its beauty, combined with the **exhilarating** experience it offers during a climb, is **incomparable** to any other adventure. Mount Everest, being the highest mountain peak, is even more attractive to **mountaineers**.

Smart Skills

Life skills — 21st Century Skills

Tara and Anika are sisters. Tara loves playing games on the computer, while Anika loves outdoor activities. During summer holidays, their family decided to go camping in the mountains. Tara would stay at the camp playing with their dog and only join the bonfire in the evening. Anika, on the other hand, tried all the camp activities. Who do you think would have enjoyed the summer holidays more? Why do you think so?

exhilarating: very happy and excited; **incomparable:** cannot be compared to any other

Famous Mountaineers

Edmund Hillary from New Zealand and **Tenzing Norgay** from Nepal were the first people to climb Mount Everest in 1953. They hoisted the Indian flag, the flag of Nepal and the flag of the United Kingdom on the summit.

Edmund Hillary and Tenzing Norgay

Bachendri Pal

In 1984, **Bachendri Pal** became the first Indian woman to climb Mount Everest. She was only 12 years old when she, along with her few friends, climbed about 3000 feet while on a picnic. She spent several weeks training—climbing hill sides, crossing rivers, running and swimming—to build her strength and stamina.

In March 1984, she began her **expedition** to climb Mount Everest from Kathmandu. One night, Bachendri was suddenly woken up. She found herself being crushed under a heavy load of something very cold. It was snow and she was caught in an **avalanche**. She was rescued by another climber, who cut open her tent with a knife and helped her out.

Many climbers were injured in that avalanche and decided to return. However, Bachendri was determined to continue and reach the peak of Mount Everest. With great determination and **grit** she reached the summit on May 23, 1984 where she proudly hoisted the Indian national flag. She and her team members were tired and shivering because of the cold, but at the same time, they were also filled with energy—the kind that comes only after achieving the greatest of feats.

Matter of Fact

Many expeditions have been made to the Mount Everest. Along the way, climbers have left oxygen canisters, broken climbing equipment and disposed of waste. The pollution has reached a critical level on the world's highest peak!

Skilling Up

Critical thinking

21ST CENTURY SKILLS

- Why are avalanches dangerous for mountaineers?
- Bachendri was saved by a friend who cut open her tent. What does this tell us about her friend? What value do we learn from the friend? Have you been in a situation where your friend has helped you? Share your experience with the class.

Arunima Sinha dared to dream the impossible as she was lying in bed after her leg had been **amputated**. She not only wanted to walk with her **prosthetic** leg but do the nearly

expedition: a short trip made for a purpose; **avalanche:** a mass of snow, rocks and ice falling quickly down a mountain; **grit:** very small pieces of stone or sand; **amputated:** cut off; **prosthetic:** artificial limb

impossible—climb the highest peak in the world, Mount Everest. This meant **rigorous** training for two years. On her expedition, she had to jump across wide gaps, which could have been fatal. However, she was **undeterred** and in 2013 she became the first female amputee to climb Mount Everest.

Arunima Sinha

Planning and Training

Extensive training for months is needed to be able to successfully climb a mountain. Training is essential for the climber to be able to cope with the severe conditions faced while climbing. Tremendous hard work, physical fitness, stamina and diet are required for mountaineering. Mountaineers go on these expeditions in teams, so that they can help each other.

Mountaineers

Mountaineers practise by climbing stairs and walking uphill with a heavy backpack. They run and cycle to build their stamina, strength and power.

Smart Skills — Information literacy (21st Century Skills)

Do you think trekking and mountaineering can damage the environment? In pairs, discuss how these adventure sports can be damaging to Mount Everest and the environment. Present your discussions to the class.

The Nehru Institute of Mountaineering in Uttarkashi and the Himalayan Mountaineering Institute in Darjeeling offer training to mountaineers. Arunima Sinha was trained by Bachendri Pal at the Uttarkashi camp of the Tata Steel Adventure Foundation in 2012.

Some of the factors that make mountaineering difficult are:

- The level of oxygen present in the air decreases at high altitudes. Therefore, the body tires easily.
- Temperature drops at high altitudes. The Himalayas are covered with snow throughout the year. This can cause high altitude sickness.

Some of the measures that mountaineers need to follow while climbing are:

- Climbers should carry all essential items in their backpacks, that should not weigh more than 15 kg. The backpack should have food, clothes, maps, water bottles, first aid kit and a waterproof jacket.
- If the climbers run out of drinking water, they can obtain water by melting snow.

rigorous: very severe; **undeterred:** to continue to do something in spite of problems

- Metal devices called **crampons** must be attached to the thick rubber boots for climbing glaciers or mountains covered with ice.
- Sleeping bags, ice axes, ropes, tents, **carabiners**, snow goggles and harnesses are some of the important equipment that the climbers must carry.

Crampons

Give It a Shot

E

- In groups, collect pictures of tools needed for mountaineering and paste them on a chart. Label the tools. You can also make a PowerPoint presentation.
- Form your own mountaineering groups in class and give your group a name. Draw a flag, symbol or a logo for your group. Make a short speech in class about your expedition.

What We Learnt

Mountaineering, river rafting, rock climbing and paragliding are some adventure sports or activities.

Edmund Hillary, Bachendri Pal and Arunima Sinha are some famous mountaineers.

Bachendri Pal was the first Indian woman to climb Mount Everest. Arunima Sinha climbed Mount Everest even though her leg had been amputated.

Mountain climbing needs a lot of hard work. Physical fitness is of utmost importance followed by stamina, medical fitness, training and diet.

Think and Answer

A. Fill in the blanks with the correct answers.

1. Bachendri Pal was .... years old when she first climbed.
   a. 15   b. 12   c. 13   d. 8
2. Edmund Hillary the first person to climb the Mount Everest was from
   a. United Kingdom   b. Australia   c. USA   d. New Zealand
3. River rafting is a .... sport
   a. Adventure   b. Indoor   c. Traditional   d. none of them

carabiner: a metal ring that can open to allow a rope to pass through, used by rock climbers to attach themselves safely to things

4. As we climb up to high altitudes the level of oxygen
   a. Increases b. decreases c. stays the same d. none of them
5. As we climb to high altitudes the temperature
   a. Increases b. decreases c. stays the same d. none of them

B. Fill in the blanks.

1. Many people find adventure sports ....
2. Ice axes, ropes, tents .... and .... are some equipment climbers must carry.
3. Arunima Sinha was trained by Baichendri Pal at the .... Foundation.
4. .... was the first Indian amputee to climb Mount Everest.
5. .... and .... are examples of adventure sports.

C. Write *T* for true and *F* for false.

1. Mountaineering does not require any training. ☐
2. Bachendri Pal was the only person on the peak when she climbed Mount Everest. ☐
3. Bachendri Pal was climbing mountains all her life and did not need any formal training. ☐
4. Climbers should carry all essential items in their backpacks, that should not weigh more than 15 kg. ☐
5. Crampons are used by the mountaineers to climb glaciers. ☐

D. Answer these questions.

1. How did Arunima prepare for the climb to Mount Everest?
2. What happened when Bachendri Pal was caught in an avalanche?
3. Why did Bachendri Pal decide to continue climbing even after the avalanche?
4. Identify and list the qualities that you see in Arunima and Bachendri.
5. What are the three facts about mountains that makes mountaineering difficult?

Cross Connect

The Himalayas are one of the many mountain ranges in the world. Some of the other mountain ranges are the Andes, the Alps, the Alaska Range, the Great Dividing Range and the Rocky Mountains. On a world map, locate these mountain ranges and in your notebook draw and colour the mountain range, name it and write the name of the country where they are located.

Web link

For more information, log on to:
https://www.natgeokids.com/uk/kids-club/cool-kids/book-club/everest/

Last accessed on 30 August 2021

20. Space Quest

Unit 6: Travel

Get Going

Floating Around

The Indian American astronaut Sunita Williams is the second woman to become the Commander of the International Space Station in 2012 where she completed 100 days. Let's read about her experience of living in space.

I love being up here and I love floating around. It took a little while to get used to falling asleep without laying down on a bed or having a pillow. Water doesn't stay at one place, it floats around as ***blob****. To wash our face or hands we had to catch these blobs and wet paper with them. Not being able to walk, we had to get used to floating around. We had to do simple things differently to stay at one place we had to strap ourselves there. Papers also had to be stuck to the wall of the spaceship. It was a lot of fun living in space, but it was difficult too.*

Discuss in the class, Sunita's experience in the spaceship.

Scientists who study space are called **astronomers**. The study of space is called **astronomy**. Let us learn more about space, the night sky and how humans travel to space.

Space

Space is a vast region beyond the Earth. All the objects that lie in space are called **celestial objects**. These include the Sun, the moon, planets, stars and several other objects made of rock, ice and fire. There is no air in space. However, it is made up of a mixture of gases.

The Solar System

The solar system consists of the Sun and eight planets. The Sun is a star made up of hot gases.

The eight planets of the solar system are **Mercury**, **Venus**, **Earth**, **Mars**, **Jupiter**, **Saturn**, **Uranus** and **Neptune**. All the planets **revolve** around the Sun in **elliptical** paths called **orbits**.

blob: a drop of a thick liquid; **revolve:** move in a circle on a central axis; **elliptical:** shape an elongated circle, stretched into an oval

Along with the eight planets, several small celestial objects are also a part of the solar system. Most planets have **satellites** that revolve around them. There are two types of satellites—**natural satellites** and **artificial satellites**. The moon is the natural satellite of the Earth. Artificial satellites are sent to space by astronauts and scientists involved in space **exploration**. Have you ever wondered how humans travel to space? Let us find out.

Solar system

Smart Skills

Information literacy

21ST CENTURY SKILLS

The Earth is the only planet in the solar system that has life on it.

- Why do you think that is possible?
- What is a Halley's comet, when will it pass the Earth next?
- Name the first artificial satellite launched by India.

Space Travel

An **astronaut** is a person who is trained to travel to space in a **spacecraft**. **Launch vehicles** or **rockets** are used to carry and place artificial satellites in the orbits of planets. These satellites, designed by humans, help scientists carry out research about space, get weather forecasts and aid communication.

Space Missions

Yuri Gagarin, a Russian astronaut, was the first human to travel to space. He took his flight on 12 April 1961 on a spacecraft named **Vostok 1**. Since then, many space missions have been carried out by different countries.

Picture Study

Where are these astronauts?
What are they talking about?

exploration: to conduct a research or as study about an unknown place

Matter of Fact

The **National Aeronautics and Space Administration (NASA)** is a United States government agency that is responsible for science and technology related to air and space. The **Indian Space Research Organisation (ISRO)** was founded in 1969 by Vikram Sarabhai.

NASA launched **Perseverance** Mars rover on July 30, 2020. It landed on February 18, 2021 on the red planet after more than 6-month voyage from Earth. China is now the second country to land rover *Zhurong* successfully on Mars on 14 May 2021.

Perseverance rover

India's space missions

Rakesh Sharma was the first Indian astronaut to travel to space on 2 April 1984. The spacecraft on which he travelled was **Soyuz T-11**.

Kalpana Chawla

Kalpana Chawla, an Indian American astronaut, was the first Indian woman to travel to space. She was one of the seven astronauts who lost their lives when their spacecraft Columbia exploded while travelling back to Earth on 1 February 2003.

Sunita Williams, an astronaut, has conducted extensive research in space.

Chandrayaan-1, India's first mission to the Moon, was an unmanned spacecraft which was launched successfully on October 22, 2008.

The Mars Orbiter Mission, also called **Mangalyaan**, a spacecraft orbiting Mars since 24 September 2014. It was launched on 5 November 2013 by ISRO.

Design engineer Muthayya Vanitha with a model of Chandryaan 2

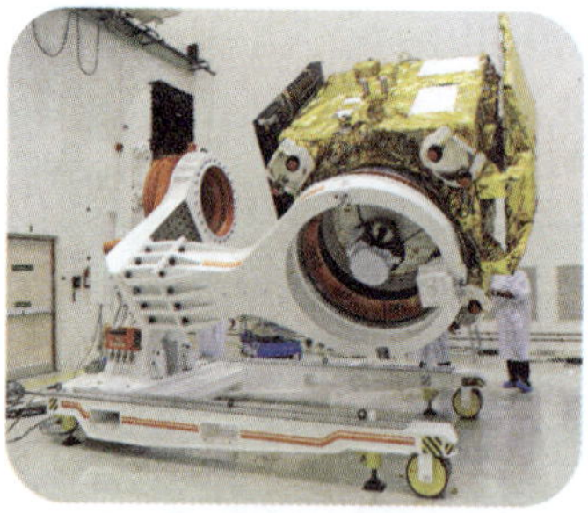
Mangalyaan

Smart Skills

Life skills

Imagine that there is no more land left on the Earth, and you with your family and friends need to move to Mars to begin a new life there. What are the things you will need to take with you, how do you think life will be on the new planet?

Space Station

A **spacecraft** in a fixed orbit around the Earth is a space station. It is a place where astronauts can live, for long time while they gather scientific data and perform experiments. The first space station was **Salyut 1**, which was launched by the Soviet Union on 19 April 1971 which fell back to Earth after only about six months. The first U.S. space station was **Skylab**, which was launched on 14 May 1973. Three separate three-person crews spent a total of 171 days there in 1973 and 1974.

Skylab space station

We know that celestial bodies are floating around in space. What keeps the moon, the Sun or the planets from falling?

Force of Gravity

We have seen a fruit or a leaf falling from a tree. When we throw a ball up in the air, why does it fall and not just stay in the air? This is because of the **force of gravity** or **gravity**. The force that attracts things to the surface of the Earth is called the force of gravity. The Earth's gravity is a force that works like a magnet.

Give It a Shot

E

- There are days when we do not see the moon, what are those days called?
- Imagine your weight is 36 kg on the Earth, what would be your weight on the moon?

When we jump in the air, we come down because gravity pulls us towards the centre of the Earth. The force of gravity depends on the distance between two objects. If the distance between the objects is more, the force of gravity is less. As a spacecraft is very far from Earth, the gravitational force of the Earth is weakened. Therefore, objects don't stay on the floor of the spacecraft, but they float. The force of gravity on Earth is six times greater than on the moon. As a result, objects weigh 6 times less on the moon than on the Earth.

Skilling Up

Critical thinking

21ST CENTURY SKILLS

- Why don't we fall off the Earth?
- Why dont the planets crash with one another?

Gravitational pull

Take a ball attached to a string. Hold the string from one end and move the ball in circular paths. Why doesn't the ball fall off? It is because your hand **exerts** a force on the string which keeps the ball from falling off. The Earth exerts a similar pull or a force towards the

exert: to apply a force

moon. It is just like moving a ball in circles, attached to an invisible string. All celestial objects exert this pull on the objects around them. This attraction between two celestial bodies is known as **gravitational pull**. The bigger the celestial object, the stronger is the pull. The gravitational pull keeps the planets in their orbits, otherwise they would just move in a straight line. The Earth's gravity makes it revolve around the Sun, just like the Sun's gravity pulls the Earth.

Day and Night Sky

What do you see in the sky during the day? We see the Sun and the clouds. All stars, including the Sun, emit light of their own. However, we can see the Sun during the day because it is very close to the Earth.

Constellation

At night, we see numerous stars in the sky. A group of stars forming a pattern when seen from the Earth is called **constellation.** The Sun makes the moon shine. The moon which shines brightly in the sky has no light of its own, it reflects the Sun's light. As the moon revolves around the Earth, only the part of the moon that faces the Sun will be lit up. The moon sometimes is perfectly round and at times, only a portion of it is **illuminated**. The different shapes of the moon that can be seen from the Earth are known as phases of the moon. When the side of the moon facing the Sun is completely illuminated, it is called a **full moon**. When the moon cannot be seen in the sky, it is because we are looking at the unlit part of the moon which is the new moon. It is called the **dark moon**. The **new moon** appears as a thin **crescent** in the sky.

Smart Skills

Digital literacy

21ST CENTURY SKILLS

Form two groups and make a PowerPoint presentation on any space mission, its importance and some interesting facts. Share it in the class.

illuminated: lighting up an object or an area

What We Learnt

Space

Space is a vast region beyond the Earth that contains all the celestial objects.

Scientists who study space are called astronomers. The study of space is called astronomy.

The solar system consists of the Sun and eight planets.

There are two types of satellites—natural satellites and artificial satellites.

The force that attracts things to the surface of the Earth is called the force of gravity.

An astronaut is a person who is trained to travel to space in a spacecraft. A spacecraft is a vehicle used for travelling in space.

Think and Answer

A. Fill in the blanks with correct answers.

1. A person who is trained to travel to space in a space craft is an .... (astronomer/ cosmonaut/ astronaut).
2. If the distance between the object is more the force of gravity is .... (more/less/same).
3. .... (Kalpana Chawla/Sunita Williams/Rakesh Sharma) was the first Indian to land on the moon.
4. .... (Sun/moon/both) are celestial objects.
5. The Earth's gravity is six times .... (less/more/equal) than that of the moon.

B. Write *T* for true and *F* for false.

1. Sunita Williams was the first person to travel to space. ☐
2. Most planets have satellites revolving around them. ☐
3. Moon is an artificial satellite. ☐
4. Our solar system consists of nine planets. ☐

C. Match the following.

1.	Natural satellite	a.	Spacecraft
2.	Rockets	b.	Yuri Gagarin
3.	Vostok 1	c.	Moon
4.	Astronaut	d.	Gravitational force
5.	Magnet	e.	Launch vehicle

D. Answer these questions.

1. What are celestial objects?
2. What is a spacecraft?
3. Name three astronauts of Indian origin who travelled to space.
4. What do you understand by the force of gravity?
5. What is the most interesting thing you see in the night sky?

Cross Connect

HC ART CC

Gravity Painting Art

Materials required: Liquid paint in various colours, card or canvas, dropper or small spoon, cups, newspaper or any thick cloth

1. Pour a different colour of paint into each cup and dilute enough so that it flows when applied to the paper.
2. Use the eyedropper or spoon to drop a few drops of colour onto the surface of card or canvas on one side of the paper using different colours in a row.
3. Tilt the paper in different directions.
4. Prop your paper against a wall. Have your newspaper or drop cloth ready to catch any spills. Drop a few drops of paint onto the surface and observe the direction of the paint.
5. Continue this until your card or canvas is covered with drips which makes designs.
6. You've now made a gravity painting!

Web link

For more information, log on to:
https://spaceplace.nasa.gov/moon-phases/en/

Last accessed on 30 August 2021

21. Magnificent Monuments

Get Going

The Great King

Rock inscription of Ashoka

Ashoka the Great was a ruler of the Maurya Empire in India with its capital in Pataliputra. King Ashoka fought many wars, but the bloodiest of them was the Kalinga War where thousands of people were killed. When King Ashoka saw all the dead bodies on the battlefield, he was filled with regret. He gave up violence and embraced Buddhism. He started building roads and hospitals for the benefit of the people and that is how he became 'Ashoka the Great'. He had a series of edicts or messages carved in stone and metal pillars and had them placed all over his kingdom. Through these edicts Ashoka taught his people to live with values, good behaviour and kindness.

One way we can learn more about the culture and history of a country is through its monuments and old buildings. These monuments tell us about the people who built them as well as about how they lived.

- Have you ever visited a monument?
- Are there monuments in your city?
- Name any monument you have heard of from your friends or family.

Our country, India, is well-known for its beautiful monuments, palaces, temples and ancient buildings. These monuments remind us of our glorious past. They are part of our **heritage**. There are several such beautiful and famous monuments all over India.

Matter of Fact

The United Nations Educational, Scientific and Cultural Organization (UNESCO) is an international organisation that protects and preserves cultural heritage around the world as World Heritage Sites. Ahmedabad is the first World Heritage City of India.

heritage: traditions, language, buildings and monuments of a particular country that have historical importance

Golden Temple

Golden Temple

The Golden Temple or Harmandir Sahib is a holy place of worship for the Sikhs located in the city of Amritsar in Punjab. It is considered a symbol of equality and togetherness.

The temple is built around a man-made pool called *sarovar*. The fifth Sikh guru, Guru Arjan, designed the Harmandir Sahib and had the *Adi Granth*, the holy book of Sikhs, kept inside the temple. The Golden Temple has four entrances which are the four directions—North, South, East, West. Thousands of people visit this holy place every day and eat **langar** in the free community kitchen, which provides free meals to all visitors without any discrimination. Maharaja Ranjit Singh had the upper floors of the Harmandir Sahib overlaid with gold foil from which it gets its name.

Smart Skills

Life skills

21ST CENTURY SKILLS

You would have seen people and children doing *seva* or volunteering to help at gurudwaras. Volunteering can be done anywhere. As a student, think of some ways you can volunteer either at home or school and discuss during **circle time**. Some ways of volunteering are, making friends with a new student in class or helping a classmate with something you are good at.

Gateway of India

Gateway of India

The Gateway of India is located on the waterfront at **Apollo Bunder** in Mumbai. It was designed by George Wittet on the visit of King George V of England and his wife Queen Mary on their first visit to India in 1911. The Gateway, however, was completed in 1924.

It is built in the shape of an arch and is 26 metres high. This structure is a beautiful mix of Indian, Arabic and Western architecture. Before Independence, this gateway served as an entry and exit point to India. It is from here that the last British ship left for England. It overlooks the Arabian Sea and is also called the 'Taj Mahal of Mumbai'.

Ajanta and Ellora Caves

The Ajanta and the Ellora caves are rock-cut Buddhist caves located in Aurangabad district of Maharashtra built 2000 years ago.

The Ajanta Caves have large prayer halls called **chaityas** and Buddhist monasteries called **viharas**. The caves were carved out of rocky hills and decorated with large paintings depicting the life of Buddha.

Ellora Caves

Ajanta Caves

About 100 km away from the Ajanta Caves are the Ellora Caves. The Ellora Caves have Hindu, Jain and Buddhist paintings and sculptures. The Hindu caves show scenes from the *Ramayana*, the Buddhist caves show the life of Buddha and the Jain caves show the various Jain saints called **Tirthankaras**. The Ellora Caves were made during the rule of the Rashtrakuta ruler, Krishna I.

Smart Skills — Information literacy (21ST CENTURY SKILLS)

The Ajanta and Ellora caves are UNESCO World Heritage Sites. In groups, bring pictures of five monuments each from different states not mentioned in this chapter. Find out the names of the monuments and the states in which they are located. On a political map of India, paste the pictures on the correct states and write the names of the monuments.

Gol Gumbaz

The Gol Gumbaz is located in Bijapur, in Karnataka and is the tomb of Muhammad Adil Shah, the Sultan of Bijapur. Gol Gumbaz means 'circular dome'. Its dome is the second largest in the world. The architecture of this monument is unique. The four towers have stairs leading to the top of the dome. The gallery around the dome provides a magnificent view of the town. The dome stands without any pillars or support.

Gol Gumbaz

Skilling Up — Problem-solving (21ST CENTURY SKILLS)

Tick the materials you think were used in ancient India to build these wonderful monuments you are learning about in this chapter. Mention the reason for your choice of materials.

Clay bricks	Stone	Steel	Cement	Mud
☐	☐	☐	☐	☐
Wood	**Lime**	**Precious gems**	**Metal**	**Leaves**
☐	☐	☐	☐	☐

Charminar

Charminar

Built by Sultan Muhammad Quli Qutub Shah in 1591, the Charminar is located in the busy Laad Bazaar in Hyderabad in Telangana. The Charminar is a beautiful piece of Indo-Islamic architecture. The name 'Charminar' comes from the four (*Char* in Hindi) minarets or minars that rise to a height of 48.7 metres. The second floor of the monument has a mosque. The Charminar looks spectacular when it is lit up at night.

Konark Sun Temple

Konark Sun Temple

Situated in the eastern part of India, in Odisha, is the famous Konark Sun Temple. The term Konark is derived from *kona* meaning corner and *arka* meaning Sun. It was built by Narasingha Deva.

The temple, dedicated to the Sun God, **Surya**, is built in the shape of a chariot—the vehicle of the Sun God. The temple is mounted on twenty-four beautifully carved wheels pulled by seven horses. It is said these wheels signify twenty-four hours of the day and the horses, the seven days of the week. The setting of the spokes in the wheels serves as sundials.

Smart Skills

Observation — 21ST CENTURY SKILLS

Look at the pictures of the Indian banknotes. The reverse side has pictures of the heritage monuments. Write the name of the monument for each banknote. Share your answers with the class.

20 .... 200 ....

100 .... 500 ....

Taj Mahal

The Taj Mahal is located in Agra in Uttar Pradesh. Built by the Mughal emperor, Shah Jahan in memory of his wife Mumtaz Mahal, the Taj Mahal is one of the New 7 Seven Wonders of the World.

Taj Mahal

To build this monument, Shah Jahan brought the best architects from around the world. Made of white marble, the Taj Mahal is built on the banks of the river Yamuna. It has beautiful gardens all around it and is surrounded by a red stone wall. Semi-precious stones are used in the floral designs to decorate the marble on the walls. It is one of the most beautiful monuments in India and looks spectacular on a full moon night.

Give It a Shot

E

These pictures are of the famous monuments of Delhi. Find out their names, who built them and when. Also, find out why they were built.

All these monuments are special and a part of our heritage. **The Archaeological Survey of India (ASI)** was established by the Government to preserve, protect, repair and maintain these monuments. Causing damage to them is a punishable offence. As students, we too can do our bit by not spitting and throwing garbage in and around the monuments, by not writing or drawing on the walls and by always buying entry tickets while visiting these monuments.

What We Learnt

India is famous for its many beautiful monuments that tell us about our country's history.

These monuments and buildings are special and part of our national heritage.

As students and citizens, we should not damage or dirty these sites when we visit them.

UNESCO protects and preserves cultural heritage around the world.

The Archaeological Survey of India preserves, protects, maintains and repairs monuments.

Think and Answer

A. Fill in the blanks.

1. The Konark Sun Temple is in ....
2. The Gol Gumbaz is the tomb of .... , sultan of Bijapur.
3. A method which each one of us can use to preserve our monuments is ....
4. The organisation which repairs and protects our monuments is called ....
5. The Taj Mahal is made of white...................................... .

B. Tick (✓) the correct answers.

1. Who built the Taj Mahal?
   a. Akbar b. Shah Jahan c. Jahangir
2. Where is the Qutub Minar located?
   a. Mumbai b. New Delhi c. Goa
3. The Gateway of India was built in the honour of ?
   a. Shah Jahan b. Emperor Ashoka c. King George V
4. Where are the Ajanta Caves?
   a. Ahmedabad b. Allahabad c. Aurangabad
5. Which of these organisations helps in preserving Indian monuments?
   a. UNESCO b. ASI c. ISRO

C. Write *T* for true and *F* for false.

1. The Charminar is a monument and a mosque.
2. The Ajanta and the Ellora caves have beautiful paintings and sculptures.
3. All old buildings are monuments.
4. The Taj Mahal was built by Akbar.
5. Guru Arjan had the gold put on the upper floors of the Golden Temple.

D. Answer these questions.

1. How did the Golden Temple get this name?
2. Who built the Charminar? Where is it located?
3. What is the differnce between Ajanta and Ellora caves?
4. Why was the Gateway of India built? Name the architect who designed it.
5. How can you, as a student, help in preserving our heritage buildings?

Cross Connect

The city of Ahmedabad and Jaipur city are world heritage cities of India. Find out the story of the city of Ahmedabad or of Jaipur. Who built the city, when and how? In groups, role-play the story of the city you have chosen and present it to the class.

Web link

For more information, log on to:
http://whc.unesco.org/en/statesparties/IN

Last accessed on 30 August 2021

22. Journey of a Seed

Get Going

Terrace Farming

Have you ever been to the hills and wondered how the people there grow crops on slopes? It is done by terrace farming. Terrace farming is the method of growing crops on sides of hills or mountains by planting on gradual terraces built into the slope. Steps known as terraces, so whenever it rains the rainwater instead of carrying away the soil nutrients down the slope flows to the next terrace. There is an outlet in each step which helps in channelising water to next step.

- Name some places in India where terrace farming method is used.

Farmers grow a variety of crops for human and animal **consumption**. Some farmers raise animals while some grow crops. They buy seeds from the market and plant them in soil. A farmer often needs a good knowledge of machines that are used on modern farms. In India, many people who live in villages are farmers and agriculture is their main occupation.

The Beginning of Farming

Long ago, humans were **hunter-gatherers**. They moved from one place to another, hunting animals and gathering plants, fruits, seeds and other edible materials. Gradually, they learnt how to plant seeds. Perhaps they observed new plants that grew from seeds that were **scattered** on the ground accidentally. With the discovery of farming, early humans stopped moving from one place to another in search of food and started living settled lives.

consumption: using up a resource; **scattered:** things thrown in different directions

Types of Crops

People grow many types of crops. Crops are classified according to the seasons in which they grow, the type of soil they need to grow, and the amount of water required to grow them.

Wheat harvest

Rabi crops are grown in winter. They are sown in late October and harvested in March or April. Wheat, mustard, barley, sesame, pulses and peas are examples of rabi crops.

Kharif crops are grown in the monsoon. They are sown between end of May and early June. Kharif crops are harvested when monsoons are over in October. Maize, gram, rice, bajra, cotton and groundnut are examples of kharif crops.

Picture Study

- While eating, have you ever wondered where your food comes from?
- Who provides us the food we eat?
- How does it come to the market?

Journey of Food

The journey of food starts from a farm. Farmers usually follow a series of steps while growing crops. These steps are also called **agricultural practices**.

Land Preparation

A farmer prepares the soil for sowing seeds by **ploughing** it. It is also known as **tilling**. Ploughing helps loosen and turn the soil. It makes the soil airy and helps the roots to **penetrate** the soil easily. It also increases the water-holding capacity of the soil. Unwanted plants or weeds are **uprooted** during ploughing. The loosened soil also helps in the growth of earthworms. Earthworms are also called 'friends of farmers' as they further turn and loosen the soil.

Ploughing

Ploughing is carried out with the help of wooden or iron ploughs, which are pulled by bullocks or buffaloes. The plough turns and breaks the soil. In large fields, tractors are used to plough the soil. The soil is then levelled with the help of a **leveller**. This prevents the soil from being eroded by wind and water.

penetrate: to go into something with force; **uprooted:** pulling a plant out of soil along with its roots

Seed Selection

It is important to select good quality seeds for sowing. Poor quality seeds do not germinate well and produce less crops. Seeds that are not damaged by insects, pests and diseases must be used by farmers.

Sowing

The process of planting seeds in the soil is known as **sowing**. This can be done **manually** or with a **seed drill**. A seed drill consists of an iron tube with a **funnel** at the top. For proper spacing of seeds, a seed drill is attached to the plough. It ensures that the seeds are sown evenly and at the right depth. It also prevents damage caused by birds and saves time and labour. Seeds of wheat, maize, bajra and mustard are sown using this method.

Seed drill

Irrigation

Crops need water to grow. In India, farmers are dependent on rainfall to water the fields. However, rainfall is irregular. Therefore, farms must be irrigated manually. The process of watering crops is called **irrigation**.

Some of the common methods of irrigation are:

Furrow irrigation: Some farmers have tube wells on their farms to irrigate their fields. A tube well pumps the groundwater to channels called **furrows** made in the fields.

Basin or flood irrigation: This is a simple method of irrigation in which a field is just filled or flooded with water.

Sprinkler irrigation: In sprinkler irrigation, water is sprayed in the fields using sprinklers. This type of irrigation is used in fields which have soil that cannot retain water. Some farmers irrigate their fields with water from tanks, open wells, canals and even lakes and ponds in their villages. The requirement of water varies with the crop and the season.

Sprinkler irrigation

manually: doing something without the help of a machine; **funnel:** a tube or pipe that is wide at the top and narrow at the bottom, used for pouring liquid into a small opening

Drip irrigation: In drip irrigation, a network of pipes or valves help distribute the water by allowing it to drip slowly to the roots of the plants. This is done either from above the soil surface or directly to the roots buried below the surface.

Drip irrigation

Manures and Fertilisers

The soil in fields become poor in its essential nutrients because of continuous farming. The requirement of nutrients is essential for the normal functioning and growth of plants. Manure and fertilisers are added to make the soil fertile. Manure is made of plant and animal waste, whereas fertilisers are made from chemicals. Manure is believed to be better than fertilisers.

Smart Skills — Communication (21st Century Skills)

- If manure and fertilisers are not added what will happen to the soil?
- How would you separate healthy seeds from damaged seeds?

Weeding

Unwanted and harmful plants that grow along with crops are called **weeds**. Removal of these unwanted plants is called **weeding**. Weeds do not allow crops to grow as they absorb all the nutrients in the soil. Weeds can be removed by hand or by using tools, such as a **trowel** or **harrow**. Some weeds are removed by using chemicals.

Harrow

Crop Protection

Crops need to be protected from insects, pests, birds and animals. Farmers spray chemicals called **insecticides** and **pesticides** to remove insects and pests from farms. A **scarecrow**, which is a dummy often in the shape of a human, is placed to scare away birds. Fencing is used to protect crops from animals.

Organic farming is a method of growing crops without using any harmful chemicals or fertilizers. The process uses natural wastes to create fertilizer for the crops. It uses natural methods of improving crop quality and quantity. Manure made from animal waste is used for increasing crop growth.

Harvesting

The process of gathering ripe crops from fields is known as harvesting. When the crops are ripe and **mature**, they are ready for harvesting. Crops should be harvested at the right time to get a good produce. Harvesting is done with the help of sickles or harvesting machines.

Skilling Up

Life skills

21ST CENTURY SKILLS

- Why are wheat grains usually washed and spread out in the sun to dry before being ground into flour?
- Why do we wash vegetables and fruits before consuming?

Harvested grains are separated from their stalks by **threshing**. This can be done with the help of animals such as bulls, camels and buffaloes who trample the grains by walking over them. Many tools and machines can also be used for threshing.

Threshing

The process of separating husk or **chaff** from the grains is called **winnowing**. A **combined harvester** is a machine that harvests, threshes and winnows the grain. Traditionally, winnowing is done by allowing grains to fall from a height. Chaff, being lighter, is blown away by the wind while the grain falls on the ground.

Give It a Shot

E

Write the names of three rabi and three kharif crops, the seasons and months in which they are sown. Write their names in your mother tongue.

	Season and Months	Crops	Names in mother tongue
Rabi			
Kharif			

Smart Skills

Information literacy

21ST CENTURY SKILLS

Different crops are grown in different parts of India. Select five crops of your choice. Find out the states in which each of these crops are grown. Use different colour codes for each crop and mark or colour in map of India.

mature: fully developed or fully grown; **chaff:** seed cases also called husks

Storing and Selling Grains

Most of the agricultural processes have been mechanised, which saves labour and time. Some farmers sell the crops to factories, where after being processed they are packed and sent to the market. Farmers dry and store their crops in gunny bags, **silos** or **godowns**. They sell it to **wholesalers**, who in turn sell it to shopkeepers. We buy cereals, pulses, vegetables and fruits from shopkeepers.

Matter of Fact

105-year-old farmer, Pappammal from Tamil Nadu was awarded the Padma Shri on the eve of Republic Day for her contribution to organic farming in the year 2021. She is an expert in organic agriculture. Pappammal cultivates millets, pulses and vegetables on her fields in Thekkampatti. She also runs a provision store and eatery.

Problems Faced by Farmers

In India, there are many farmers who do not own land or fields. They are **landless farmers**. They work on farms owned by others to earn a living. They do all the work on the fields, right from sowing seeds and harvesting to threshing. They are **daily wage labourers** and get paid by the day. On days when there is no work on the fields, they must look elsewhere for work and money.

Smart Skills

Digital literacy

21ST CENTURY SKILLS

- Collect newspaper articles about farmers of India and problems they face.
- Which kind of modern machines make farmer's work easier?
- Find out about stubble burning and its impact. In a group of three, a PowerPoint presentation on any one topic and present the report in class.

Some farmers own small pieces of land and sell most of the crop for money to take care of the needs of their family. They are called **subsistence farmers**. Subsistence farmers often borrow money from local moneylenders to buy agricultural tools, seeds, fertilisers, and pesticides. If their crops fail because of less rainfall or because of poor quality seeds, the farmers cannot return the money to moneylenders. In **distress**, many farmers finally sell their land and migrate to the cities in search of a better life.

Subsistence farmer

silo: a tall tower on a farm used for storing grain; **godown:** a building where grains are stored; **wholesalers:** shopkeepers who sell a product at cheap prices; **distress:** in suffering and pain

What We Learnt

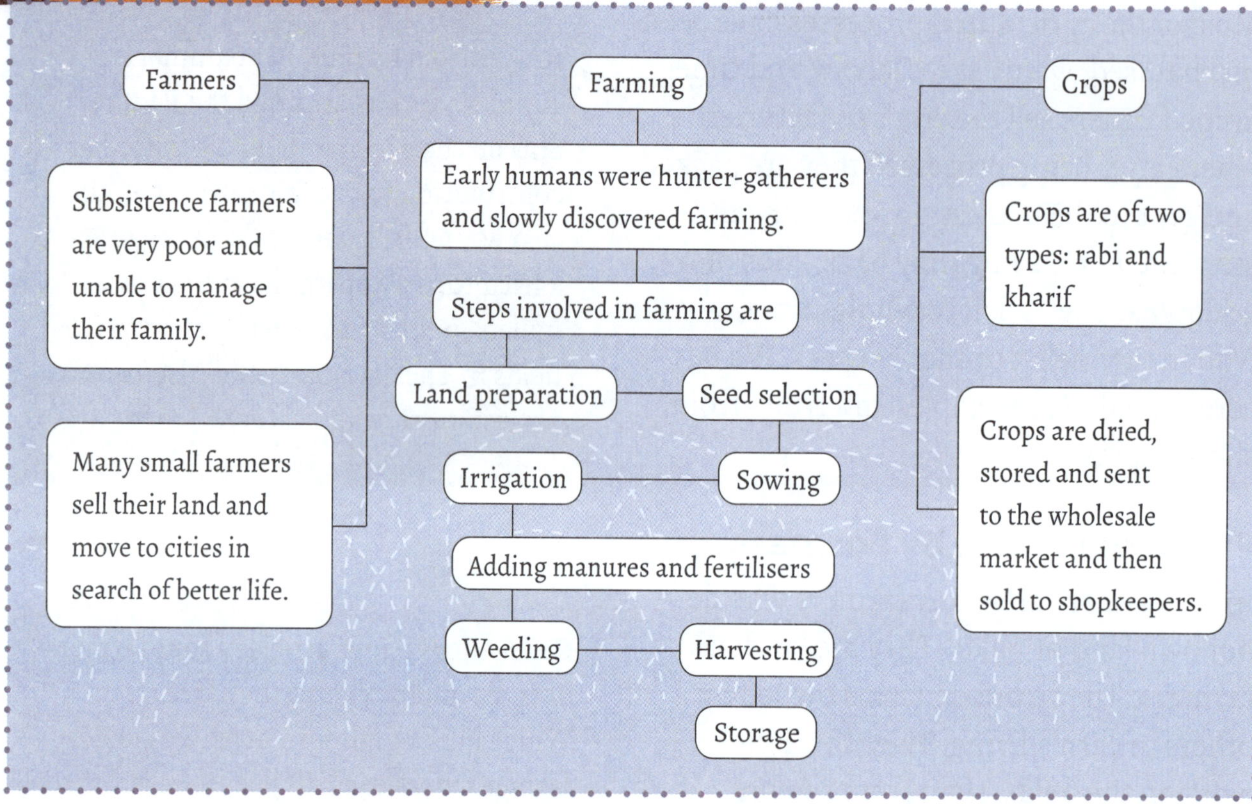

Think and Answer

A. Fill in the blanks.

1. The process of planting seeds in soil is known as ....
2. .... is the process of separating grains from stalks.
3. .... are very poor and unable to manage their family needs.
4. Winnowing is the process of separating .... from grains.
5. Soil is levelled with the help of ....

B. Fill in the blanks with the correct answers.

1. The land where crops are cultivated is known as a.. .

   a. court　b. field　c. meadow　d. farm

2. Removal of unwanted plants is called ....

   a. seeding　b. breeding　c. weeding　d. tricking

3. Sowing can be done manually or with the help of a.. .

   a. drill machine　b. seed drill　c. hammer drills　d. trowel

4. Adding fertilisers and manure make the soil ....

   a. sterilized　b. fertile　c. harder　d. inferior

C. Unscramble these words.

1. FRKHAI ....
2. ENARUM ....
3. VELELREL..
4. HOULPG ....
5. GINFMAR ....

D. Answer these questions.

1. How is land prepared for farming?
2. Why is weeding necessary for farming?
3. What is organic farming?
4. What is harvesting?
5. What are the problems faced by landless farmers?
6. Why are earthworms known as 'friends of farmers'?
7. Why are manures believed to be better than fertilisers?

Cross Connect

- Collect one recipe of food items each from any three states of India share it with the class.
- List five rabi crops and kharif crops each. Name the states and places where they are grown and mark them on a map of India.

Web link

For more information, log on to:
https://www.nationalgeographic.com/foodfeatures/green-revolution/

Last accessed on 30 August 2021

Suggested Assessment 1

Maximum Marks: 60

A Fill in the blanks with the correct answers. 10

1. A seed germinates when it gets the right amount of .... (air and water/air, water and sunlight/air, water, sunlight and warmth).
2. Farmers who do not own their own land are called .... (small/landless/daily wage) farmers.
3. Lotus and water lily are examples of .... (submerged plants/rooted floating plants/free-floating plants).
4. .... (cats and dogs/lizards and cats/lions and cats) can smell with their tongues.
5. One of the traditional games of India is .... (cricket/kite flying/hockey).
6. Work done by a person to earn money for a living is called a .... (job/service/volunteering).
7. Wind pipe is also known as .... (bronchi/trachea/alveoli).
8. Swollen and bleeding gums are symptoms of .... (scurvy/kwashiorkor/goitre).
9. The characteristics that are passed down from one generation to another are called .... (hereditary/acquired/habit).
10. Animals who feed on other animals are called .... (carnivores/omnivores/herbivores).

B Fill in the blanks. 5

1. Eye colour is an example of .... trait.
2. Plants that obtain nutrition by growing on other plants are called .... plants.
3. .... is a game played with two sticks.
4. Taking in air through the nose or mouth into the lungs is called ....
5. Services that affect our daily lives are called .... services.

C Match the following. 5

1. Photosynthesis	a. Traits
2. Cotyledons	b. Seed coat
3. Distinct characteristics	c. Taekwondo
4. Testa	d. Seed leaves
5. Martial arts	e. Food

D Give reasons. 10

1. Plants and animals depend on each other.
2. New relations are formed once a child is born.
3. Migration that takes place only in a particular season.
4. Dolphins keep coming out of water.
5. We should show respect to those who help us.

E Write *T* for true or *F* for false. 5

1. Coffee grows on small areas called plantations.
2. Nocturnal animals depend on their sense of smell.
3. The right lung is larger than the left lung.
4. Rice is grown in West Bengal, Punjab, Assam and Kerala.
5. Social work is done to earn money.

F Answer these questions. 20

1. How do families help shape our values?
2. Why is seed dispersal important for plants?
3. Do all plants grow from seeds? Explain with the help of two examples.
4. What is interdependence?
5. What is the difference between games and sports?
6. How do animals sleep?
7. What are the symptoms and diagnosis of dengue?
8. Why should we practise deep breathing exercises?
9. How do development projects lead to migration?
10. Differentiate between manual and intellectual labour.

G Draw and label the stages of germination. 5

Suggested Assessment 2

Maximum Marks: 60

A Fill in the blanks with the correct answers. **5**

1. The Konark Sun Temple is built in the shape of a .... (sun/chariot/dome).
2. Storage tanks built deep in the ground are also called .... (baolis/pulley/spring).
3. Yuri Gagarin took his flight on 12 April, 1961 on a spacecraft named .... (Vostok-1/Soyuz T-11/Zhurong).
4. .... (first aid/treatment/medicine) is the immediate help given to the injured.
5. The process of separating husk or chaff from the grains is called .... (threshing/winnowing/harvesting).

B Write *T* for true or *F* for false. **10**

1. Microbes can be seen only by the naked eye. ☐
2. Ants use a special chemical to communicate with each other. ☐
3. The Taj Mahal was built by Muhammad Adil Shah. ☐
4. Excessive rainfall can cause a cyclone. ☐
5. CNG is used only as a domestic fuel. ☐
6. The process of digestion starts even before the food enters the mouth. ☐
7. Mountaineers go on climbing expeditions in teams. ☐
8. Tents protect people from heavy snowfall. ☐
9. In distress farmers sell their land and migrate to the cities. ☐
10. Freshwater is found in oceans and seas. ☐

C Fill in the blanks. **5**

1. When food is exposed to air or moisture for a long time, it gets ....
2. Natural gas is found along with .... in oil wells.
3. People who live around our house are our ....
4. The process of planting seeds is called ....
5. .... operations are carried out after a disaster.

D Give one word for the following. 5

1. When animals of the same species interact with each other, the behaviour they exhibit is called ....
2. Sri Harmandir Sahib is popularly called the ....
3. A piece of wood or a scale kept to support a broken bone is called ....
4. All the planets revolve around the Sun in elliptical paths called ....
5. The process of watering crops is called ....

E Find the words in the word grid with the help of the clues. 5

P	E	T	R	O	L	E	U	M	U
R	E	S	P	R	I	N	G	I	S
O	K	U	T	C	H	A	Z	C	A
T	O	N	O	M	A	D	S	R	R
I	P	A	L	A	F	O	I	O	O
E	E	M	U	N	T	H	L	B	V
N	H	I	R	R	I	G	O	E	A
S	C	A	R	A	B	I	N	E	R

Clues

1. They are necessary for growth and repair of the body ....
2. It is a type of a crude oil ....
3. Tiny living thing which cannot be seen ....
4. Great ocean waves ....
5. They use tents as houses ....
6. Farmers store their crops in huge metal container called ....
7. Houses not structurally strong and often need repairing ....
8. A metal ring used by climbers that opens to allow a rope to pass through ....
9. A man-made pool built near temples ....
10. A flow of groundwater that emerges naturally on the Earth's surface ....

F Read the paragraph and answer the questions. 10

Satyajit lives in Orissa where due to floods, their house is submerged in water. They are all on the rooftop of their house waiting for help. He is an animal lover and thinks about animals living in the forest. How do animals in the forest protect themselves?

1. Humans on the rooftop waiting for the animals to join them.
2. Animals will climb on the trees to save themselves.
3. Animals can sense danger and will move to higher levels, where there is less water.
4. Animals will fight with each other and drown.

G Give reasons. 5

1. Carpooling can help us conserve fuel.
2. When we jump in the air we come down.
3. Water is scarce even though there is water in the seas and oceans.
4. Houses in plains have flat roofs.
5. We should not waste food.

H Answer these questions. 10

1. Why do we need to preserve food?
2. How do members of honeybee family communicate with each other?
3. Name two vehicles that do not use fuels. Explain how these vehicles move,
4. Why are kutcha houses built in villages?
5. What would happen if there was no force of gravity?
6. What are some of the factors that make mountaineering difficult?
7. How do fuels cause pollution?
8. What steps should we take during an earthquake?
9. How are tube wells and wells used by farmers for irrigation?
10. Why is the Konark Sun Temple built in the shape of a chariot?

I Draw and label the diagram of the human digestive system. 5

Notes

Notes